Presented To

From

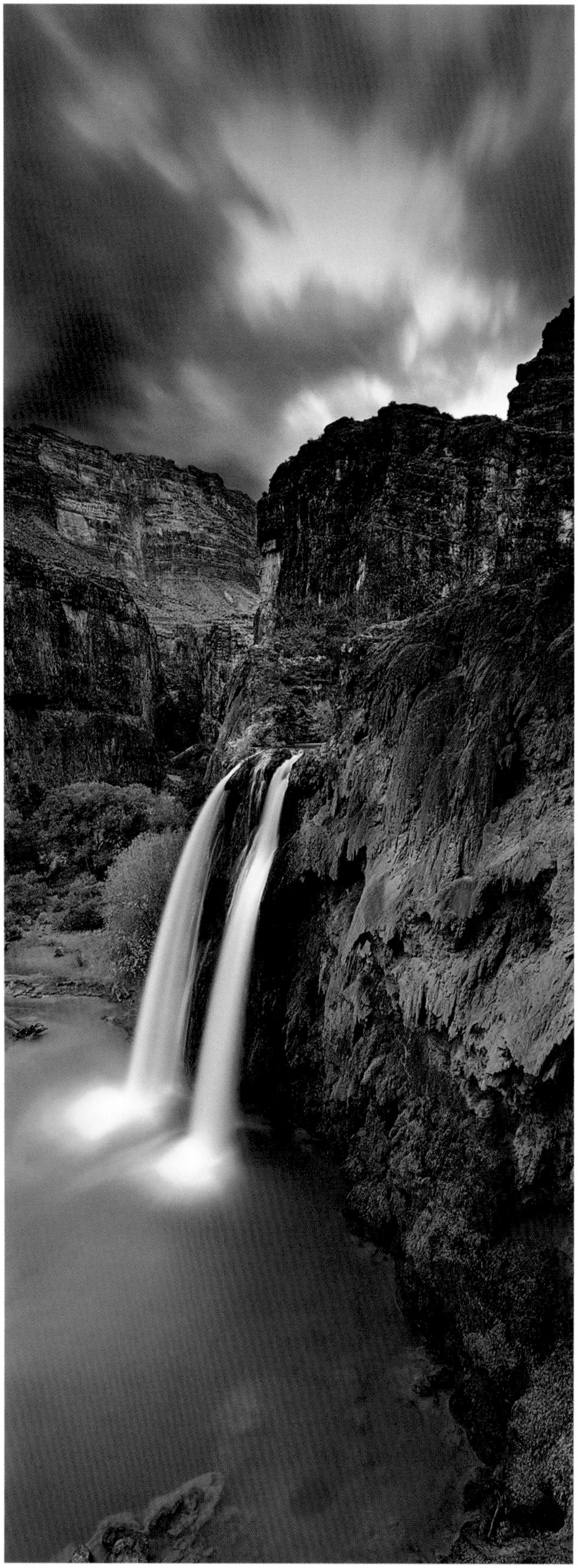

Havasu Falls, Grand Canyon, Arizona

WALKING WITH GOD IN
AMERICA

THE HEART OF AMERICA IN WORD AND IMAGE

PANOGRAPHS® BY

KEN DUNCAN

THOMAS NELSON
Since 1798

NASHVILLE DALLAS MEXICO CITY RIO DE JANEIRO BEIJING

Published in Nashville, TN, by Thomas Nelson. Thomas Nelson is a trademark of Thomas Nelson, Inc.

Thomas Nelson, Inc., titles may be purchased in bulk for educational, business, fundraising, or sales promotional use. For information, please email SpecialMarkets@ThomasNelson.com.

Designed by Brand Navigation

ISBN: 978–14041–0513–3

Printed in China

Reflections, Williamsville, Vermont

COVER PHOTO: I found this barn near Williamsville, Vermont, and thought it would look lovely at sunrise. Next day, on my way to the location, I was listening to a Christian radio station while a preacher was speaking about how we often are too casual in asking God for help with little things like parking spaces or weather conditions when God is busy dealing with major issues. At the time I felt rather convicted, as I quite often speak to God about all sorts of things, including parking spaces, but God has always been faithful even with the small matters.

When I arrived at the barn it was blowing a gale, but I needed the reflection in the pond to make it really work. I sat there for hours hoping for a change in the weather, until a wild horse came along and tried to push me and my camera into the pond. I was finally able to get the horse to leave me alone, and then I started to reflect on what the preacher had said. As a father, I know that if it was within my power to help my daughter with something—even the smallest thing—I would do it. If I, an earthly father, love to do whatever I can for my child, surely it follows that God would be even more willing to help His children. So I asked God to help me with the wind. Immediately there was a calm that lasted for two minutes—just long enough for me to get the photo. I guess that radio preacher was just having a bad day. My heavenly Daddy loves me and is interested in even the smallest matters of my life.

WITH [GOD] ARE

WISDOM AND STRENGTH,

He has counsel and understanding. . . .

He makes nations great, and destroys them;

He enlarges nations, and guides them.

— JOB 12:13, 23

Contents

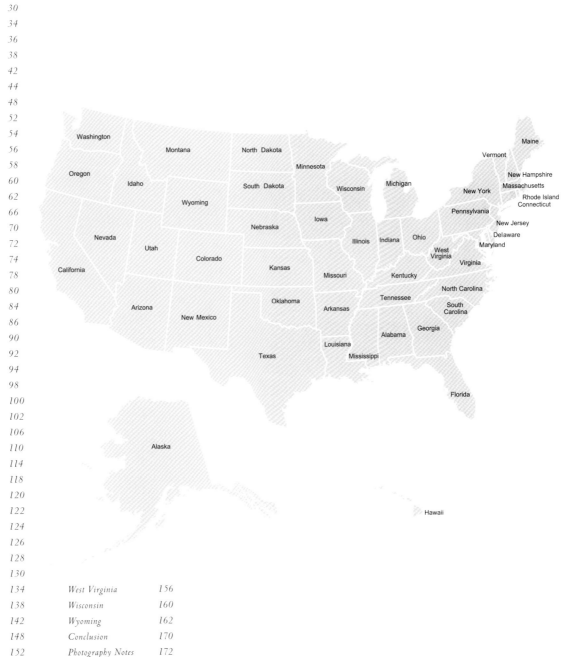

Washington
Montana
North Dakota
Minnesota
Maine
Vermont
Oregon
Idaho
South Dakota
Wisconsin
Michigan
New Hampshire
Massachusetts
New York
Rhode Island
Connecticut
Wyoming
Iowa
Pennsylvania
Nebraska
New Jersey
Delaware
Nevada
Illinois
Indiana
Ohio
Maryland
Utah
West Virginia
Colorado
Virginia
California
Kansas
Missouri
Kentucky
North Carolina
Tennessee
Oklahoma
South Carolina
Arizona
Arkansas
New Mexico
Georgia
Alabama
Louisiana
Texas
Mississippi
Florida
Alaska
Hawaii

Introduction

It might seem funny that although I am Australian, God has given me a real burden for America. No nation in the world has been more naturally blessed than the United States, and I believe God has done that so people will understand how much He cares for the nation. America's faith in God is what has made it one of the greatest countries on earth, and that faith is a beacon of hope for other struggling nations around the world.

One of the things that motivated me most to do this book was that God clearly showed me how the enemy was trying to undermine America's godly foundation. He showed me that the awakening of the battle would be when the government is pressured to remove the words "In God We Trust" from the currency. This is something Christians must never allow to happen. Throughout my journey I was aware of many instances where the enemy was trying to remove the Ten Commandments from public buildings and stop prayer in schools, and at times I was deeply saddened. It is so important for America to stand strong against all the attempts to exclude God from people's lives, including government.

In January 1838 in a church in Springfield, Illinois, Abraham Lincoln delivered a speech wherein he warned his nation of approaching danger.

> "At what point shall we expect the approach of danger? By what means shall we fortify against it? Shall we expect some transatlantic military giant to step the ocean, and crush us at a blow? Never! All the armies of Europe, Asia and Africa combined, with all the treasures of the earth (our own excepted) in their military chest; with a Bonaparte for a commander, could not by force, take a drink from the Ohio, or make a track on the Blue Ridge, in a trail of a thousand years.

> "At what point then is the approach of danger to be expected? I answer, if it ever reach us, it must spring up amongst us. It cannot come from abroad. If destruction be our lot, we must ourselves be its author and finisher. As a nation of free men, we must live through all time, or die by suicide."

When I first heard this speech of Abraham Lincoln's narrated, it touched me deeply. I felt as if the enemy of which he spoke was lurking in the shadows here and now, in the form of apathy, hopelessness, fear, and division, and that his speech was a warning cry from the past. The United States of America displays the words "In God We Trust" on its currency, but has the nation's trust in the steadfast God been exchanged for the ever-changing passions of humanity? The Civil War in America gave testimony to the terrible cost of division. The 2000 and 2004 presidential elections showed how divided a nation could be when its hope is placed in mere mortals. A house that is divided can fall. Is there still trust in the Highest power, or are we placing our hope in human authority?

The United States of America has been blessed beyond measure. No nation has been granted a more beautiful place to call home. I believe God has blessed this country so that it may be a beacon to others by upholding the belief that liberty, faith, hope, and unity can conquer any adversity. The bounty of awesome natural wonders is a constant reminder that there is accountability to a power higher than oneself. My prayer is that the American people never forget where their help comes from—the Maker of heaven and earth.

Our roots provide the strength to withstand the storms of constant change. A hardy breed of men and women pioneered this great nation of America and bequeathed to all a land of hope and possibility—a land of freedom. They have shown the way to overcome obstacles and stand strong in times of adversity. Now is a time for all Americans to focus on where they have come from and what the foundation for the future will be.

I journeyed through this land on a three-year pilgrimage endeavoring to capture the spirit of America. My aim is to show the awesome power of God through the beauty of His creation, for I believe that it is the foundation of trust in God that has made America such a blessed nation. I hope the images in this book touch your heart.

Ken Duncan.

KEEP THE CHARGE of the LORD your God:

to walk in His ways, to keep His statutes,

His commandments, His judgments, and His testimonies...

that you may prosper in all that you do and wherever you turn.

—I KINGS 2:2–3

THE
NORTH
FACE

IT CANNOT BE

EMPHASIZED TOO STRONGLY

or too often that this great nation was founded, not by religionists, but by Christians; not on religions, but on the gospel of Jesus Christ. For this very reason peoples of other faiths have been afforded asylum, prosperity, and freedom of worship here.

—*Patrick Henry,* Revolutionary Patriot (1736-1799)

FOUR FREEDOMS:

The first is freedom of speech and

expression—everywhere in the world. The second is

freedom of everyone to worship God in his own way,

everywhere in the world. The third is

freedom from want...everywhere in the world.

The fourth is freedom from fear...

anywhere in the world.

—*Franklin D. Roosevelt,* U S. President (1933-1945)

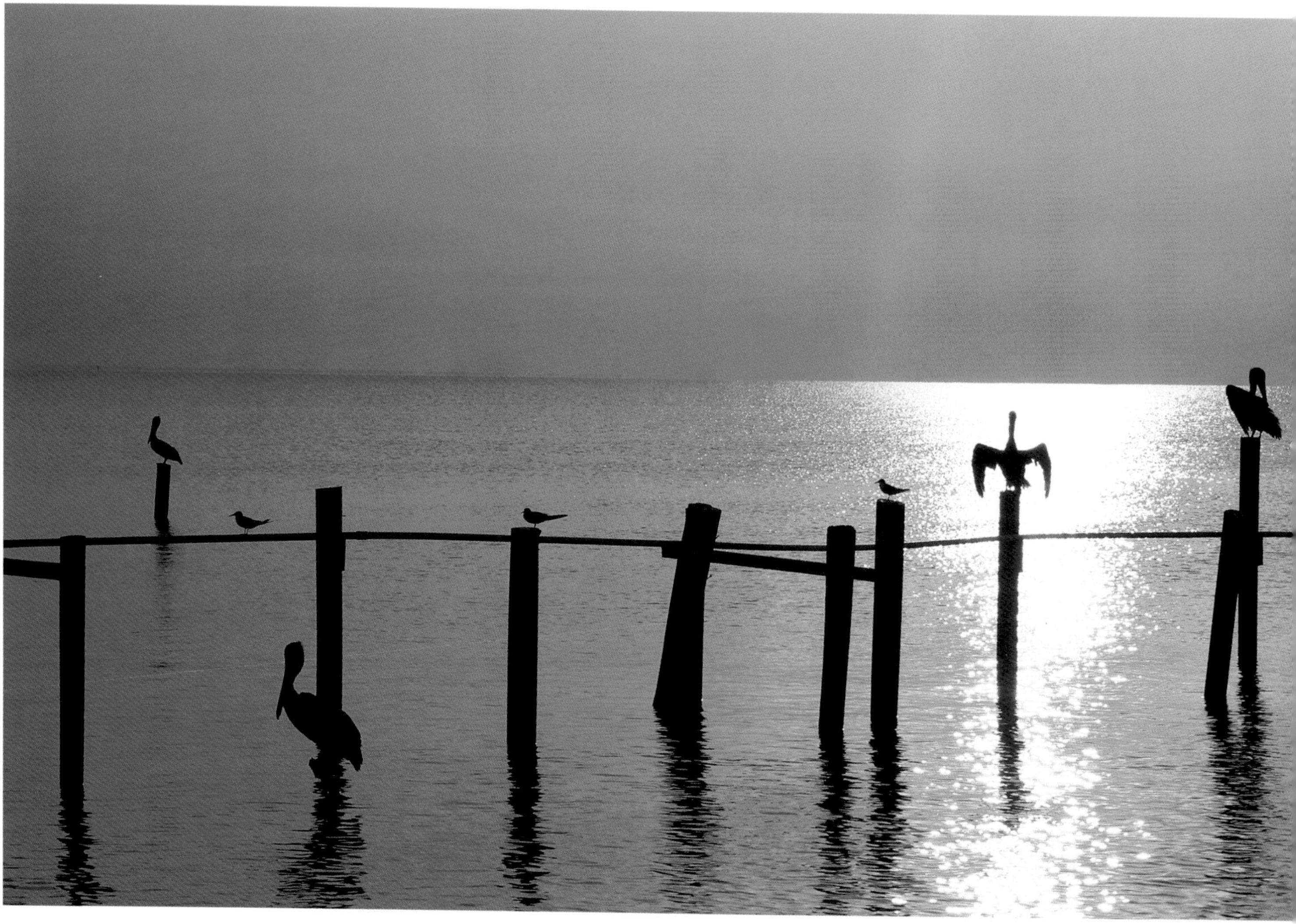

"FROM THE RISING OF THE SUN even to its going down,

My name shall be great among the Gentiles;

In every place incense shall be offered to My name,

And a pure offering;

For My name shall be great among the nations,"

Says the LORD of hosts.

MALACHI 1:11

Heron Bay, Alabama

A wonderful bird is the pelican—its beak can hold more than its belly can! Here at Heron Bay the pelicans await the returning fishermen, along with any morsels they might glean during the cleaning of the catch.

The best and most beautiful things in the world cannot be seen or even touched.
They must be felt within the heart.

— *Helen Keller, Advocate for the blind, born 1880 in Tuscumbia, Alabama*

I WILL BLESS THE LORD who has given me counsel;

My heart also instructs me in the night seasons.

I have set the LORD always before me;

Because He is at my right hand I shall not be moved.

PSALM 16:8

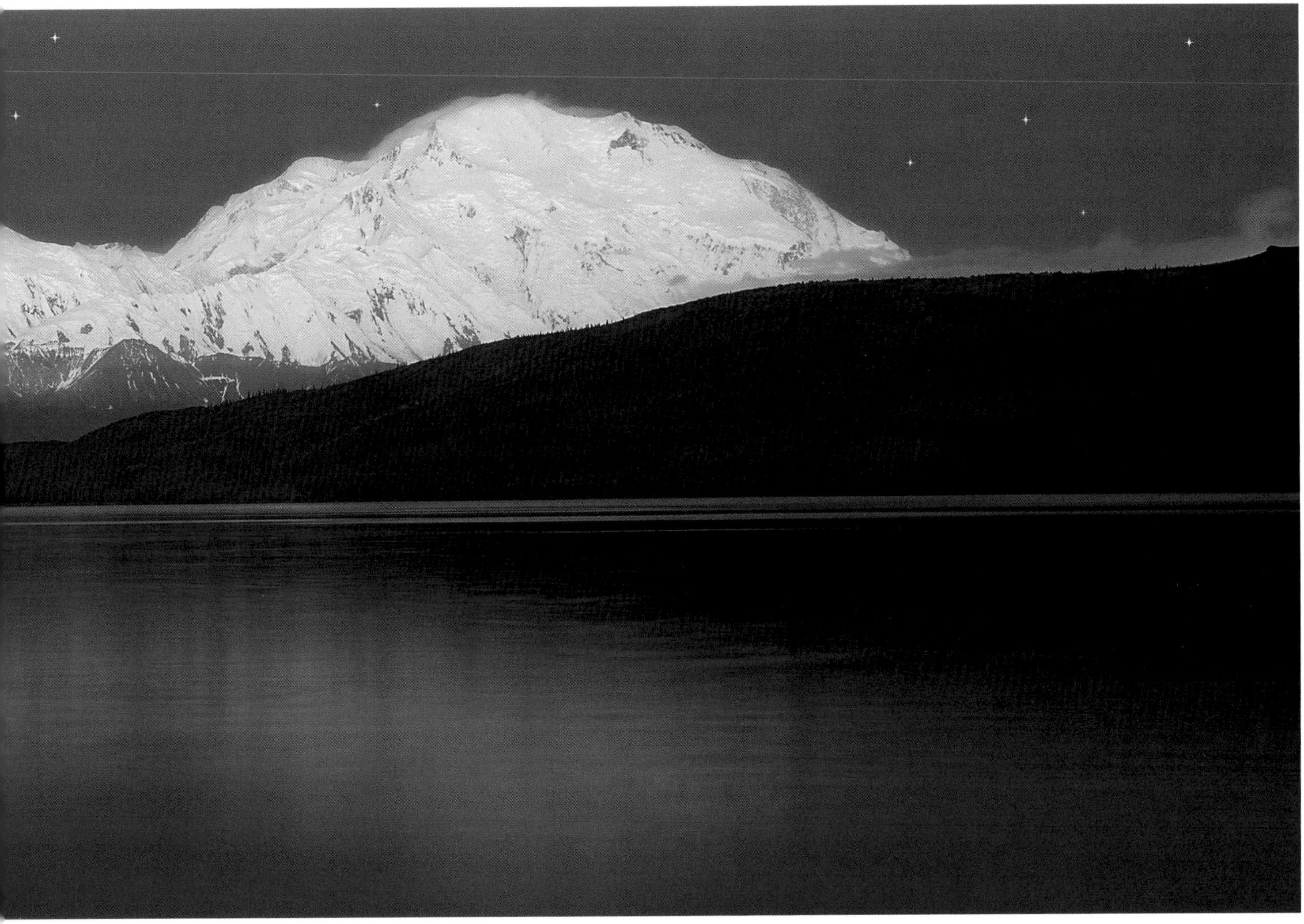

Wonder Lake, Denali National Park, Alaska

The vastness of Alaska cannot compare to the immensity of God. His love is stronger than the mountains, His treasures are richer than the gold fields, His purity is whiter than the snow.

THE WORKS OF THE LORD ARE GREAT,

Studied by all who have pleasure in them.

His work is honorable and glorious,

And His righteousness endures forever.

He has made His wonderful works to be remembered;

The LORD is gracious and full of compassion.

PSALM 111:2-4

Moonlit Majesty, Denali National Park, Alaska

Alaska is known as "The Last Frontier" for its unspoiled wilderness, but it was part of the first frontier for passing anti-discrimination laws in the United States. A Tlingit couple, Roy and Elizabeth Peratrovich, led the struggle to achieve equal rights for native Alaskans, and on February 16, 1945, nineteen years before Congress enacted the Civil Rights Act of 1964, the state of Alaska passed a law providing all citizens with full and equal enjoyment of public accommodations. Elizabeth's powerful testimony before Alaska's senators is credited as one of the primary reasons for that victory. That night, Roy and Elizabeth went dancing in a hotel where the day before they were not welcome. Their victory reminds us that America offers hope that a few Christians really can make a difference.

Alaska

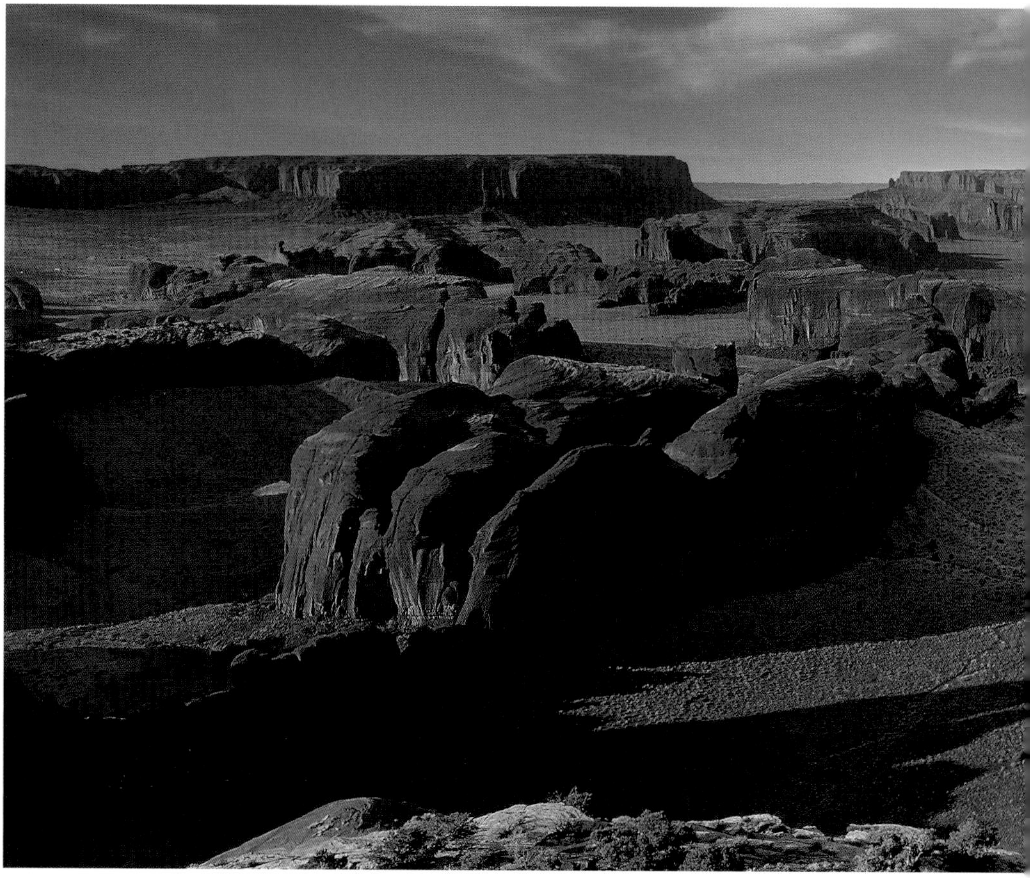

JESUS STOOD AND CRIED OUT, SAYING,

"If anyone thirsts, let him come to Me and drink.

He who believes in Me, as the Scripture has said,

out of his heart will flow rivers of living water."

JOHN 7:37-38

View from Hunts Mesa, Monument Valley, Arizona

In Monument Valley I was overwhelmed by the spectacular display of God's handiwork, and I felt a real burden to pray for America to overcome the spiritual attacks it is facing. I felt God's pain over what has been happening to a nation He holds dear to His heart, and I began to wonder, "God, will they ever be able to stop this enemy trying to remove You as their foundation stone?" God spoke clearly to my heart and said, "It's okay, Ken. My followers will wake up and stand up. There is going to be revival in this nation. The Navajo people who are connected to this land you are seeing will be part of that revival. There will be signs, wonders, and miracles, and one of the signs will be that wells of this area that have dried up will once again flow." I had begun to wonder if my attempts to remind Americans of God's greatness through evidence of His handiwork was maybe a waste of time, but suddenly I knew there was hope. The God in whom America trusts will be victorious!

IF MY PEOPLE who are called by My name
will humble themselves,
and pray and seek My face,
and turn from their wicked ways,
then I will hear from heaven,
and will forgive their sin
and heal their land.

2 CHRONICLES 7:14

Horseshoe Bend, Colorado River, Arizona

When I saw this place I was fascinated—it reminded me that God allows U-turns. We can sometimes be heading in the wrong direction and then we turn around and things work out right.

HE SHALL BE LIKE A TREE

Planted by the rivers of water,

That brings forth its fruit in its season,

Whose leaf also shall not wither;

And whatever he does shall prosper.

PSALM 1:3

Arkansas

With over 600,000 acres of lakes, 9,700 miles of streams, millions of acres of forests, and two mountain ranges, Arkansas is known as "The Natural State." More than a million gallons of hot water flow daily from the springs in Hot Springs National Park, and Crater of Diamonds State Park is the world's only diamond mine that's open to the public. God has poured rich blessings indeed on this country!

Duty, Honor, Country. Those three hallowed words reverently dictate what you ought to be, what you can be, what you will be.

— *General Douglas MacArthur,*
Born 1880 in Little Rock, Arkansas

OZARK NATIONAL FOREST, ARKANSAS

GOD, WHO IS RICH IN MERCY,

because of His great love with which He loved us,

even when we were dead in trespasses,

made us alive together with Christ (by grace you have been saved),

and raised us up together, and made us sit together

in the heavenly places in Christ Jesus.

EPHESIANS 2:4-6

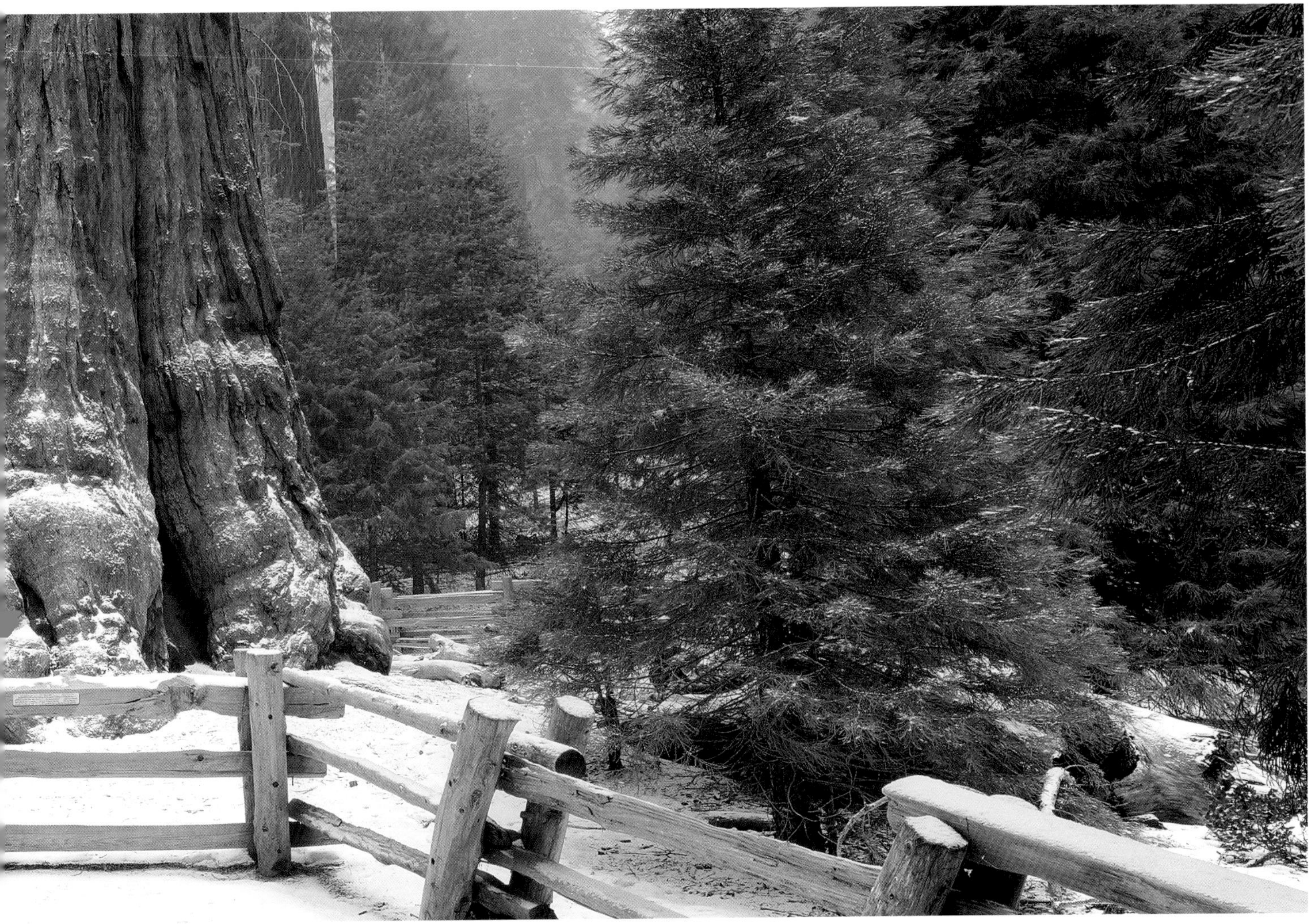

General Sherman Tree, Sequoia National Park, California

How can anyone not believe in God when they see these giant sequoia trees? Here you see a person completely dwarfed by the immensity of the tree. We are blessed God loves us so much! Who is man compared to the awesomeness of God? And we are only a small part of His diverse creation.

GARRAPATA STATE PARK, CALIFORNIA

America! America!
God shed his grace on thee
And crown thy good with brotherhood
From sea to shining sea!

—*Katharine Lee Bates*

"From sea to shining sea" became a reality on September 9, 1850, when California was admitted as the 31st U. S. state.

HE SHALL HAVE DOMINION FROM SEA TO SEA

and from the river unto the ends of the earth.

PSALM 72:8

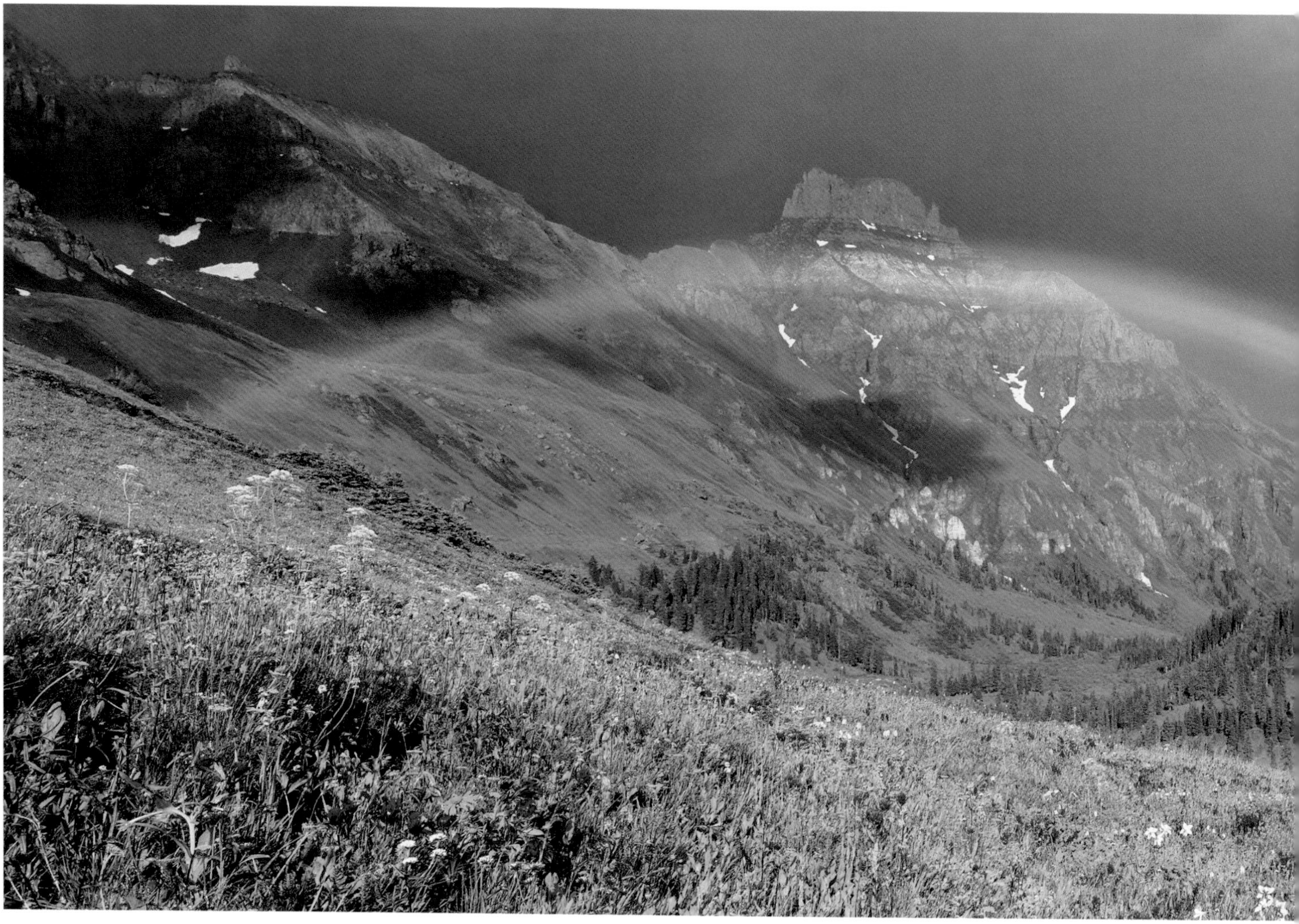

AND GOD SAID: "This is the sign of the covenant which I make between Me and you,

and every living creature that is with you, for perpetual generations:

I set My rainbow in the cloud, and it shall be for the sign of the covenant between Me and the earth.

It shall be, when I bring a cloud over the earth, that the rainbow shall be seen in the cloud;

and I will remember My covenant which is between Me and you and every living creature of all flesh."

GENESIS 9:12-15

Rainbow, Yankee Boy Basin, Colorado

I had found a beautiful location for that quintessential shot of wildflowers in a mountain setting, but circumstances were not going well. First the morning light was bland. Then it began to rain. There I sat under a huge multi-colored umbrella looking very obviously like an idiot in a field getting rained on. Two hours passed, and I suggested to God that maybe we could have a little rainbow. After all, nothing is impossible with God! Suddenly there was a huge clap of thunder that made my hair stand on end. Ten minutes later the clouds parted slightly, the sun broke through, and a marvelous rainbow appeared over the field of wildflowers. It was breathtaking—far more spectacular than I had dared to imagine. The moral of this story is have faith. We often need to stand firm through the storms until the blessing comes, as it takes a little rain to bring forth rainbows in our lives.

UNCOMPAHGRE NATIONAL FOREST, COLORADO

We can all pray. We all should pray.

We should ask the fulfillment of God's will. We should ask for courage, wisdom,

for the quietness of soul which comes alone to them

who place their lives in His hands.

— *Harry S Truman, U. S. President (1945-1953)*

SING, O HEAVENS, for the LORD has done it!

Shout, you lower parts of the earth;

Break forth into singing, you mountains,

O forest, and every tree in it!

For the LORD has redeemed Jacob,

And glorified Himself in Israel.

ISAIAH 44:23

THOSE WHO GO DOWN TO THE SEA IN SHIPS,

Who do business on great waters,

They see the works of the LORD,

And His wonders in the deep. . . .

Oh, that men would give thanks to the LORD for His goodness,

And for His wonderful works to the children of men!

PSALM 107:23-24, 31

SUNSET, OLD MYSTIC SEAPORT, CONNECTICUT

Mystic Seaport has been a maritime center for America since the 1600s. For the first three hundred years, it was filled with bustling shops and shipyards filled with wooden vessels, but as railroads and steamships grew in prominence, the traditional industry declined. In 1929, three men launched a preservation effort to make sure the area's rich seafaring history wasn't lost. Today Mystic Seaport continues to thrive as a popular destination both for research and for tourism.

> If you ask an American, who is his master? He will tell you he has none,
> nor any governor but Jesus Christ.
>
> —*Governor Jonathan Trumbull, Born 1710 in Lebanon, Connecticut*

A MAN'S HEART PLANS HIS WAY,

But the LORD directs his steps.

PROVERBS 16:9

Sunrise, Bethany Beach, Delaware

I love the simple majesty of this scene. Before the sun rose, the horizon was just a haze of misty cloud and the view almost featureless. But then the sun began its ascent. Normally there are only a few moments to shoot a rising sun before it becomes too bright and blows out the shot, but here the cloud acted like a giant diffuser, allowing me to capture an awesome display of golden light. I shot many frames here, but this one is my favorite. The positioning of the waves gives great balance to the image—one wave broken, one wave breaking, and one that's yet to come. To me, it's like the Father, Son, and Holy Spirit, a reminder of God's loving presence in a moment of great simplicity.

I WILL BOTH LIE DOWN IN PEACE, and sleep;

For You alone, O LORD,

make me dwell in safety.

PSALM 4:8

Siesta Beach, Sarasota, Florida

Siesta Beach . . . how appropriate the name. Imagine lying back on a big deckchair, sunglasses in place, ready to drift off into dream time. Never get so busy making a living that you forget to make a life!

I love this shot of a lifesaver's hut. On the sign it says, "No lifeguard on duty," and the number of the hut is "3." It reminds me that my lifeguards—the big Three: Father, Son, and Holy Spirit— are always on duty.

FOR LO, THE WINTER IS PAST,

The rain is over and gone.

The flowers appear on the earth;

The time of singing has come,

And the voice of the turtledove

Is heard in our land.

SONG OF SOLOMON 2:10-11

Azaleas, Florida

Florida's name literally means "flowery." When Juan Ponce de León discovered Florida in 1513 while searching for the Fountain of Youth, he landed just a few days after Easter. He named the land *La Pascua Florida,* or "Flowery Easter," in honor of the Spanish Easter feast.

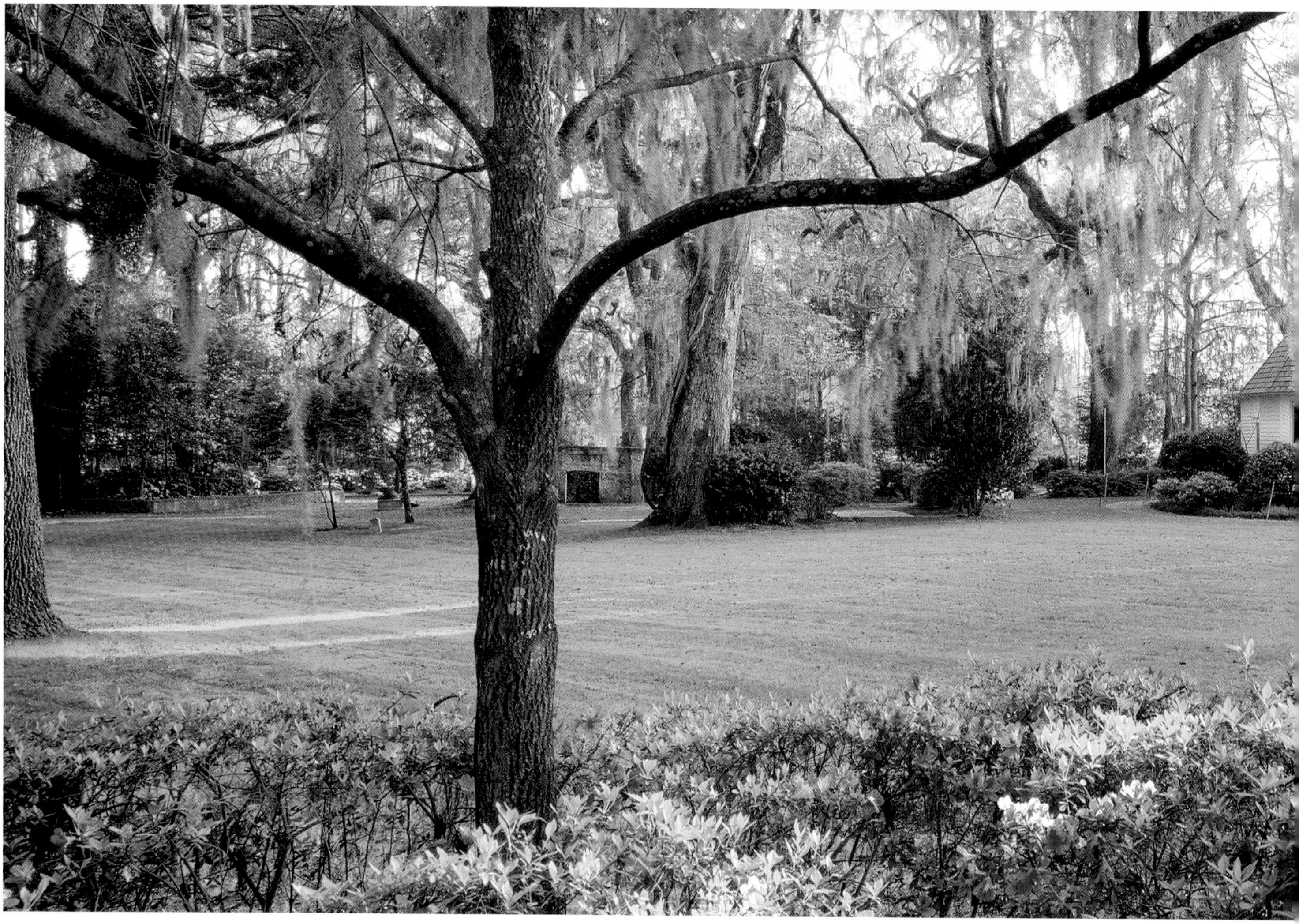

PRAISE THE LORD!

Sing to the LORD a new song,

and His praise in the assembly of the saints.

PSALM 149:1

Christ Church, Saint Simmons Island, Georgia

The Saint Simons Island mission was established in 1736 by brothers John and Charles Wesley, who ministered to the first English settlers on the island before they returned to England, where they founded the Methodist Church. Today the picturesque Saint Simons church still serves the people of the island.

Come, Thou almighty King, Help us Thy Name to sing, help us to praise!
Father all glorious, o'er all victorious, Come and reign over us, Ancient of Days!

—*Charles Wesley, chaplain for James Oglethorpe's second colony in Georgia, 1736*

I WILL POUR WATER

on him who is thirsty,

And floods on the dry ground;

I will pour My Spirit on your descendants,

And My blessing on your offspring;

ISAIAH 44:3

Wailua Falls, Kauai, Hawaii

The "Fantasy Island" waterfall is just one of the wonders of this island paradise, and it reminds me of the innumerable blessings God has poured out upon America and its people. His love is Paradise!

FROM THE RISING OF THE SUN

to its going down

The LORD's name is to be praised.

The LORD is high above all nations,

His glory above the heavens.

PSALM 113:3-4

Bali Hai, Kauai, Hawaii

Hawaii is known as the "Aloha State," a moniker proudly adopted in honor of its distinctive native word used both for greetings and goodbyes. Translated, *aloha* generally means "love" or "compassion" or "peace." The state motto is *Ua mau ke ea o ka aina I ka pono*, which means, "The life of the land is perpetuated in righteousness."

YOU CROWN THE YEAR WITH YOUR GOODNESS,

And Your paths drip with abundance.

They drop on the pastures of the wilderness,

And the little hills rejoice on every side.

The pastures are clothed with flocks;

The valleys also are covered with grain;

They shout for joy, they also sing.

PSALM 65:11-13

Hay Rolls, Mica, Idaho

If we look to the answer as to why, for so many years, we achieved so much, prospered as no other people on earth, it was because here, in this land, we unleashed the energy and individual genius of man to a greater extent than has ever been done before. Freedom and the dignity of the individual have been more available and assured here than in any other place on earth. The price for this freedom at times has been high, but we have never been unwilling to pay that price. . . . We are too great a nation to limit ourselves to small dreams.

—*Ronald Reagan, U. S. President (1981-1989).*

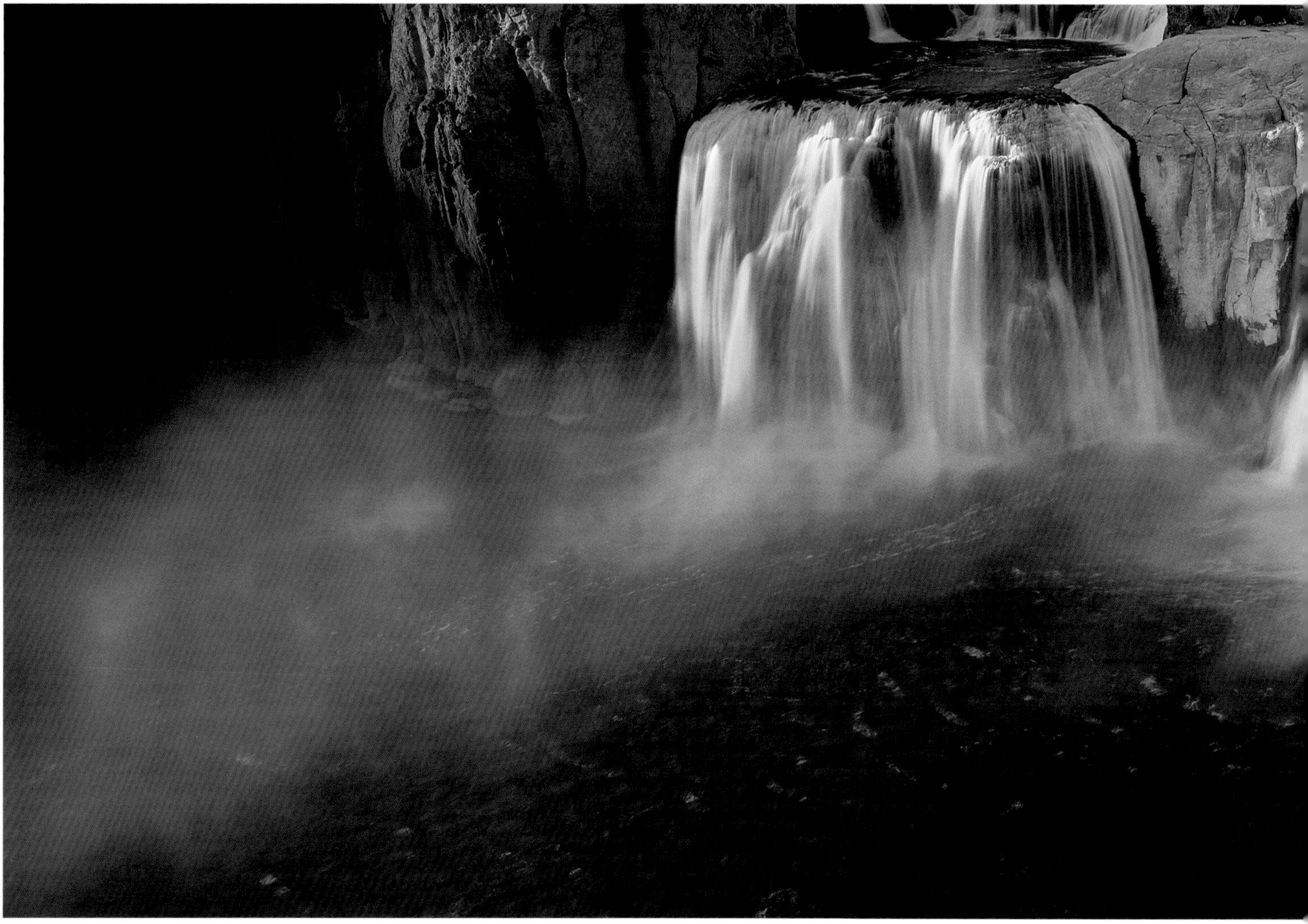

DEEP CALLS UNTO DEEP

at the noise of Your waterfalls;

All Your waves and billows have gone over me.

The LORD will command His lovingkindness in the daytime,

And in the night His song shall be with me—

A prayer to the God of my life.

PSALM 42:7-8

Shoshone Falls, Idaho

Shoshone Falls is among the most spectacular of natural beauties along the Snake River. At 212 feet, the falls are higher than Niagara Falls. They are best viewed during the spring, when water flows are high. During some other times of the year the falls are all but dry as the water is diverted for agricultural use. What a blessing—having an abundance of water for both beauty and service!

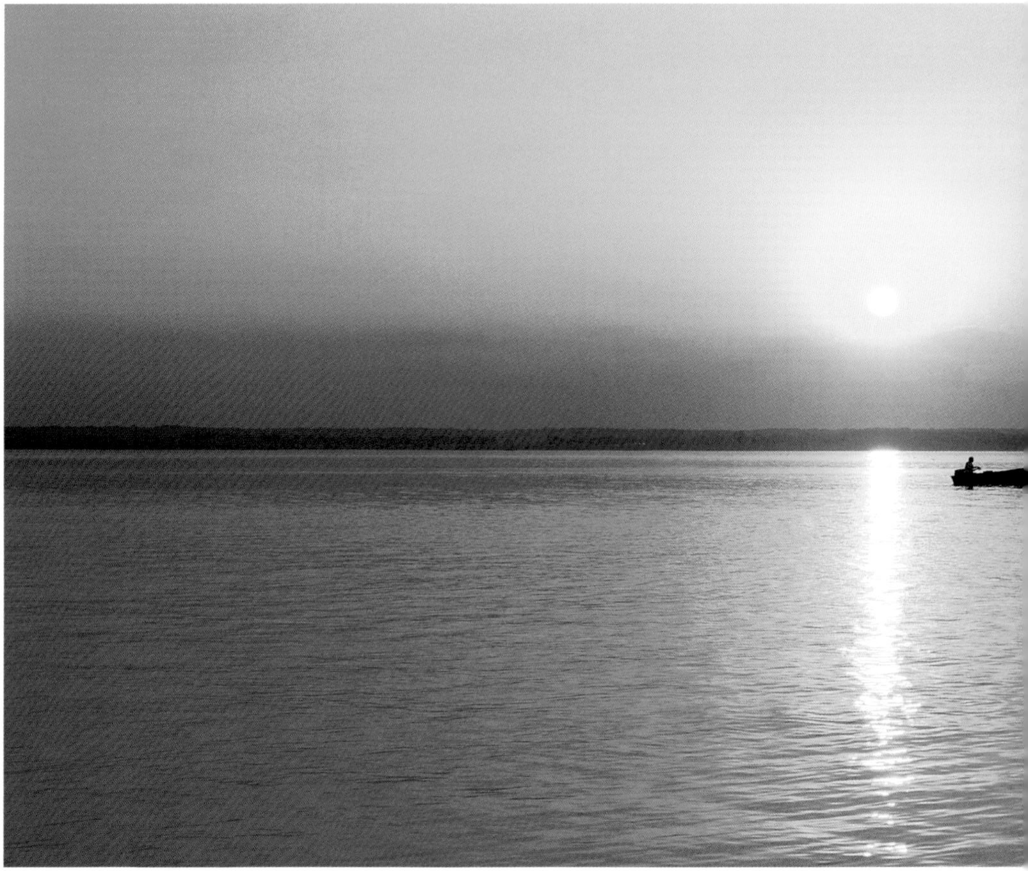

IN CHRIST WE ARE SET FREE

by the blood of his death, and so we have forgiveness of sins.

How rich is God's grace, which he has given to us so fully and freely.

EPHESIANS 1:7-8 NCV

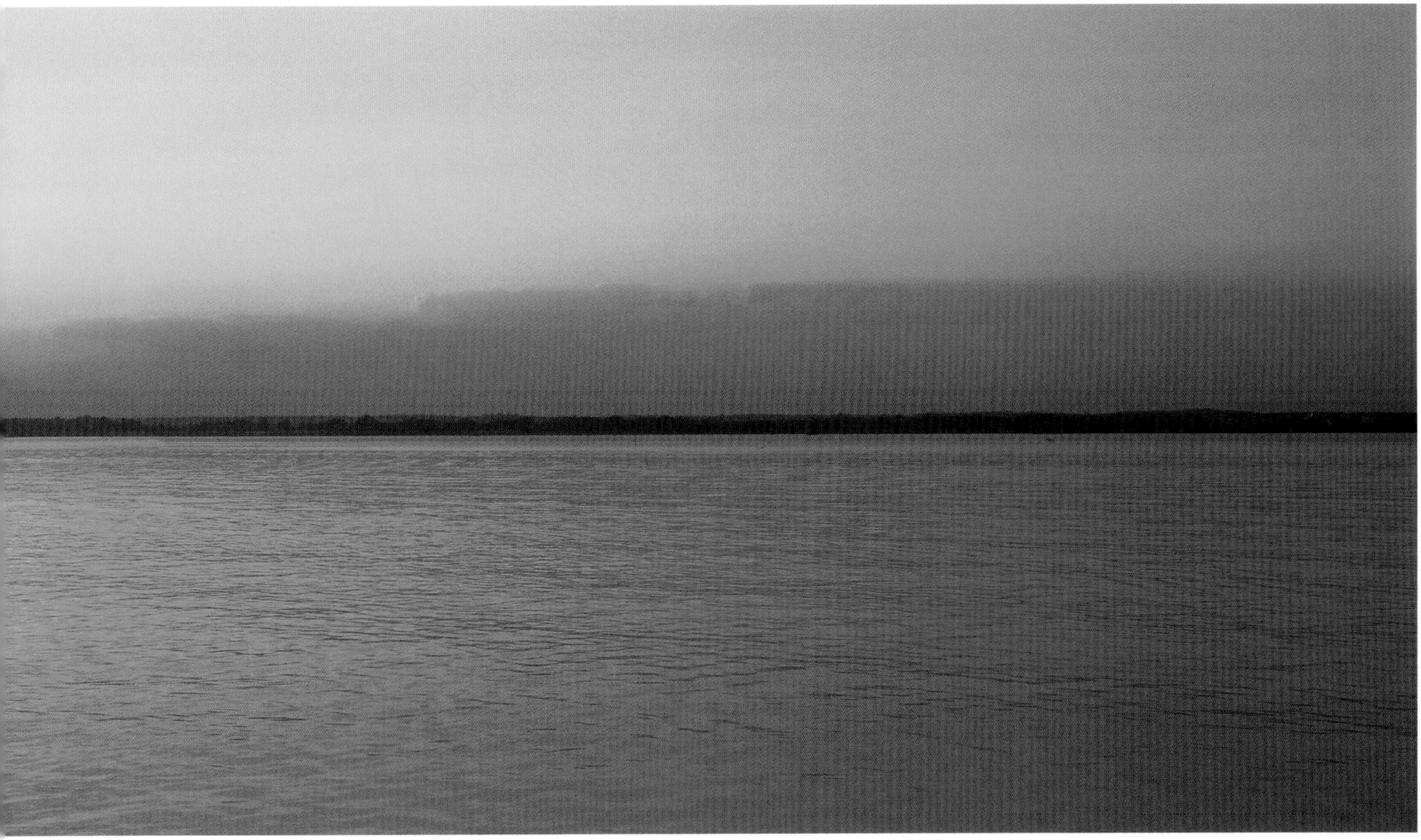

Mississippi River, Nauvoo, Illinois

With malice toward none, with charity for all, with firmness in the right as God gives us to see the right, let us strive on to finish the work we are in, to bind up the nation's wounds, to care for him who shall have borne the battle and for his widow and his orphan, to do all which may achieve and cherish a just and lasting peace among ourselves and with all nations.

—*Abraham Lincoln*. U. S. President (1861-1865)
Hometown: Springfield, Illinois

FOR WE KNOW that if our earthly house, this tent, is destroyed,

we have a building from God, a house not made with hands,

eternal in the heavens. . . . So we are always confident,

knowing that while we are at home in the body we are absent from the Lord.

For we walk by faith, not by sight.

2 CORINTHIANS 5:1, 6-7

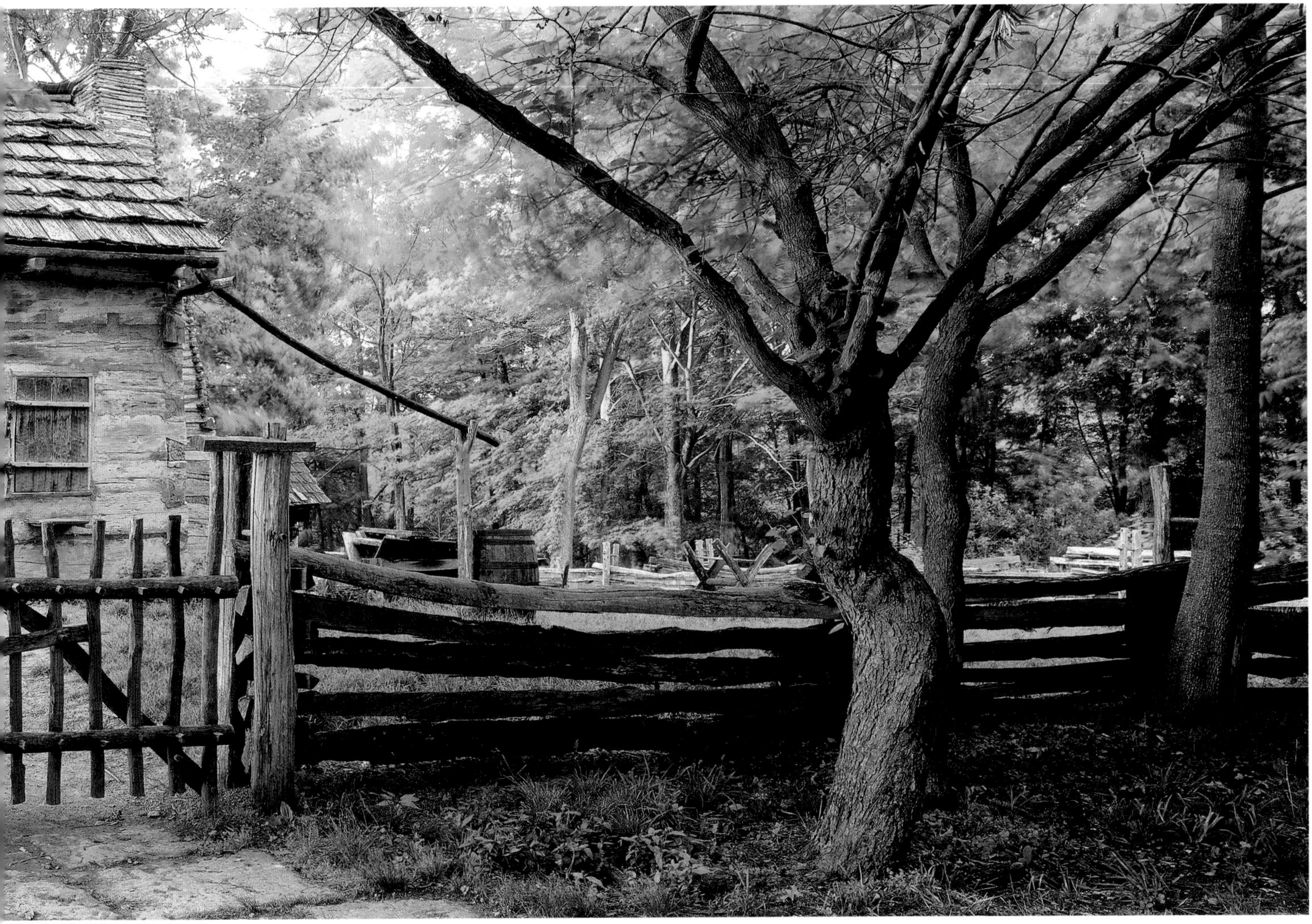

Lincoln Boyhood National Memorial, Lincoln City, Indiana

No other people have a government more worthy of their respect and love
or a land so magnificent in extent, so pleasant to look upon,
and so full of generous suggestion to enterprise and labor.

—*Benjamin Harrison,* U.S. President (1889-1893)
Hometown: Indianapolis, Indiana

A DAY IN YOUR COURTS is better than a thousand.

I would rather be a doorkeeper in the house of my God

Than dwell in the tents of wickedness.

For the LORD God is a sun and shield;

The LORD will give grace and glory;

No good thing will He withhold

From those who walk uprightly.

PSALM 84:10-11

Marion Lutheran Church, Gunder, Iowa

The questions before our country are problems of progress to higher standards; they are not the problems of degeneration. They demand thought and they serve to quicken the conscience and enlist our sense of responsibility for their settlement. And that responsibility rests upon you, my countrymen, as much as upon those of us who have been selected for office. Ours is a land rich in resources; stimulating in its glorious beauty; filled with millions of happy homes; blessed with comfort and opportunity. In no nation are the institutions of progress more advanced. In no nation are the fruits of accomplishment more secure. In no nation is the government more worthy of respect. No country is more loved by its people. I have an abiding faith in their capacity, integrity and high purpose. I have no fears for the future of our country. It is bright with hope.

— *Herbert Hoover,* U. S. President (1929-1933), born 1874 in West Branch, Iowa

THE WISDOM THAT is from above is first pure, then peaceable, gentle,

willing to yield, full of mercy and good fruits,

without partiality and without hypocrisy.

Now the fruit of righteousness is sown in peace

by those who make peace.

JAMES 3:17-18

Sunflower Sunrise, Goodland, Kansas

The Kansas state flower is the wild sunflower. In the early fall, the roads of Kansas are ablaze with brilliant yellows. Nearly three thousand years ago Native Americans domesticated the sunflower for food. Lewis and Clark even made mention of how they were used by the plains Indians. Lined up like a thousand suns, the golden prairies stretch toward the open sky in the heart of America.

I had been told the best time to go to Kansas to see the sunflowers in bloom, but when I arrived even a few days before the recommended date, I was too late. The heads on all the sunflowers had drooped and their petals had begun to wither. I felt a gentle voice urging me to ask a local farming supplier whether any sunflowers were still standing tall. He remembered a farm that had been hit by a tornado just after the fields were sown, and the farmer had replanted, which made the crop late. This photo is in that field. Thank God for the farmer's tenacity in replanting!

Cumberland Falls, Kentucky

Sometimes we envisage how things should be and are disappointed when they don't work out. I had gone to Cumberland Falls for a beautiful sunrise. It never happened. I could have been impatient and left, but I relaxed and waited. Conditions changed and I was rewarded with this shot. Moods and emotions are ever-changing. None will last forever. They are like the weather that comes and goes in a pattern beyond our control. Patience and a positive attitude help us live in the here and now and appreciate every moment.

LIKE THE APPEARANCE of a rainbow in a cloud on a rainy day

so was the appearance of the brightness all around it.

This was the appearance of the likeness of the glory of the LORD.

EZEKIEL 1:28

HOW LOVELY are your tents, O Jacob!

Your dwellings, O Israel!

Like valleys that stretch out,

Like gardens by the riverside,

Like aloes planted by the LORD,

Like cedars beside the waters. . . .

Blessed is he who blesses you,

And cursed is he who curses you.

NUMBERS 24:5-6, 9

Atchafalaya Swamp, Louisiana

It's well before sunrise as we start our adventure into the bayou. Our guide has taken us through a maze of channels—too many twists and turns for me to have any idea where we are. As the light begins to penetrate the swamp, ghostly trees take form like menacing giants with outstretched arms. An old abandoned hunting platform makers me wonder what happened to the hunter. Strange noises—slithering and gurgling—greet the day. The swamp is alive and well.

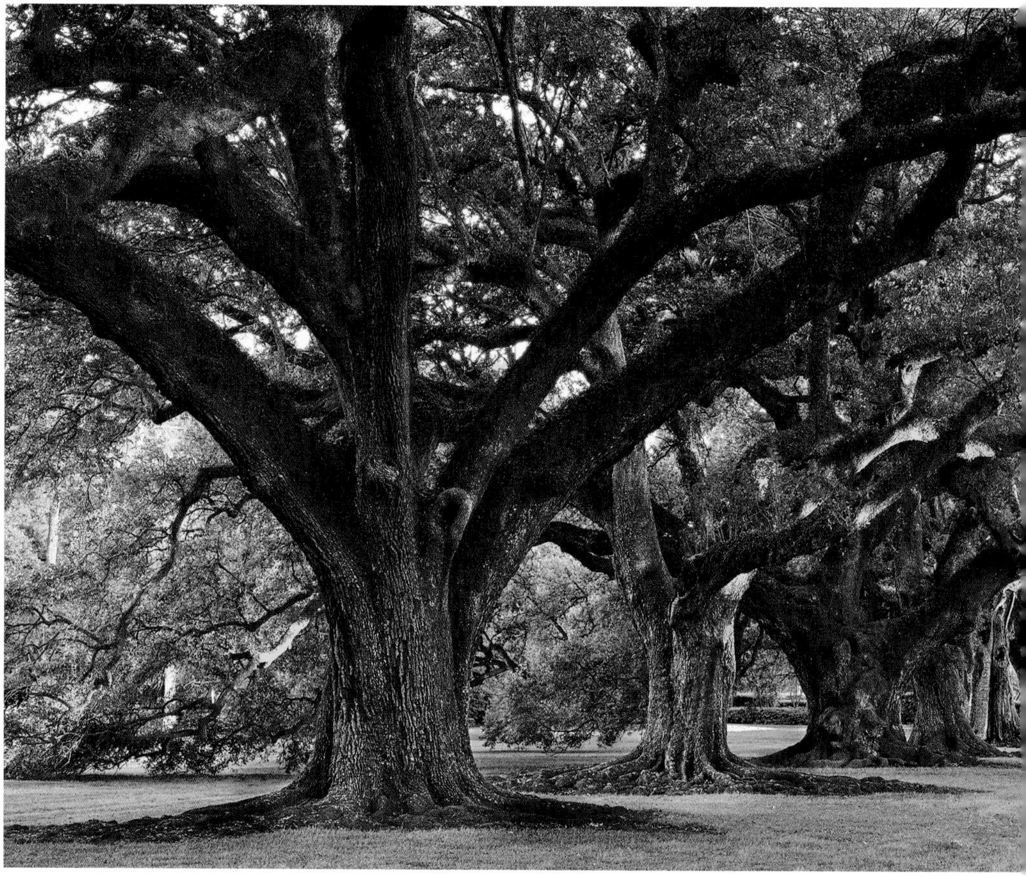

PRAISE THE LORD!

Blessed is the man who fears the LORD,

Who delights greatly in His commandments.

His descendants will be mighty on earth;

The generation of the upright will be blessed.

Wealth and riches will be in his house,

And his righteousness endures forever.

PSALM 112:1-3

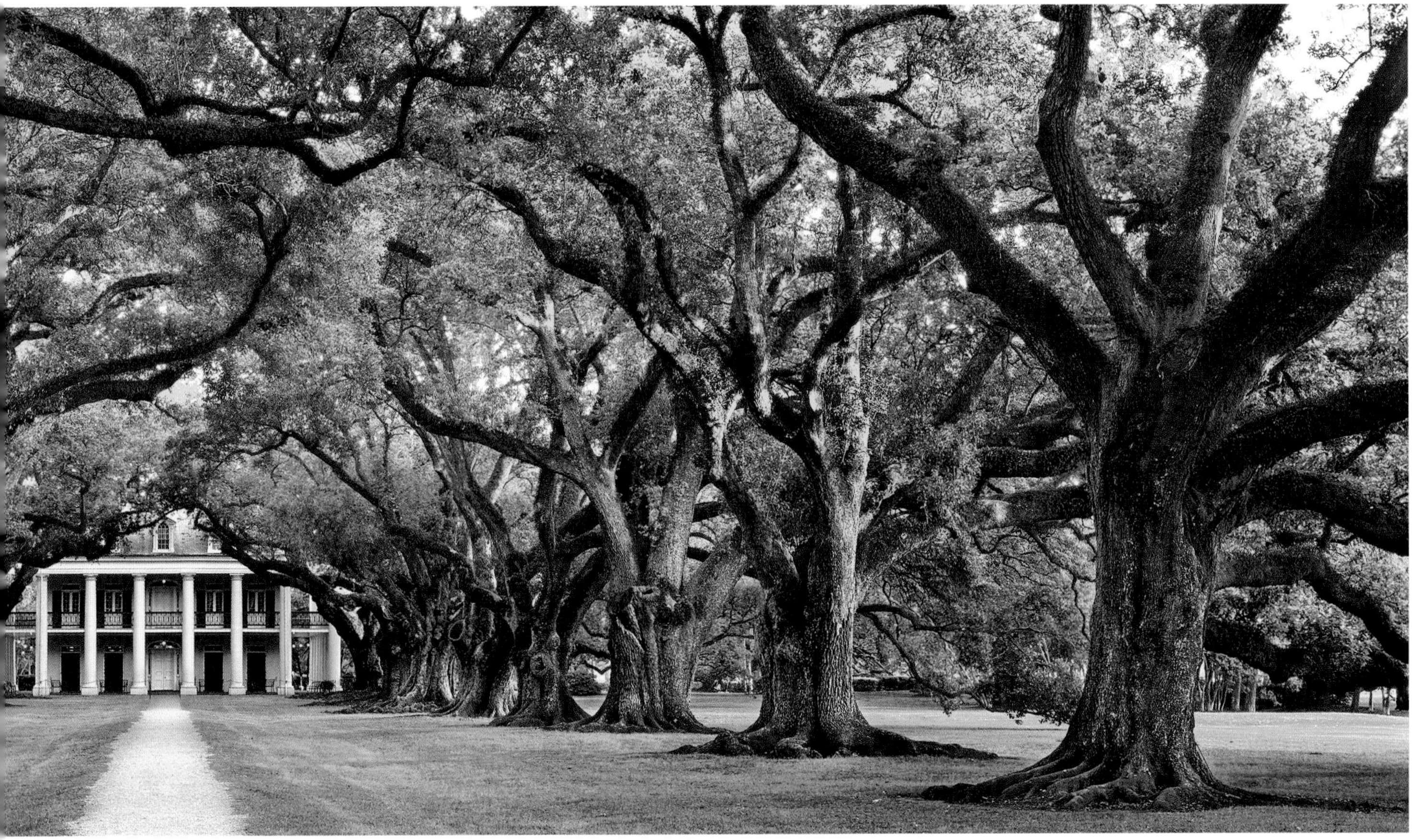

Oak Alley Plantation, Vacherie, Louisiana

This distinguished landmark is named after the impressive rows of mighty oaks planted in the eighteenth century before the plantation home was built. The alley of trees leads to the great Mississippi River. The plantation has seen both years of prosperity and years of adversity, just as happens with people, and its endurance inspires as much as its beauty does.

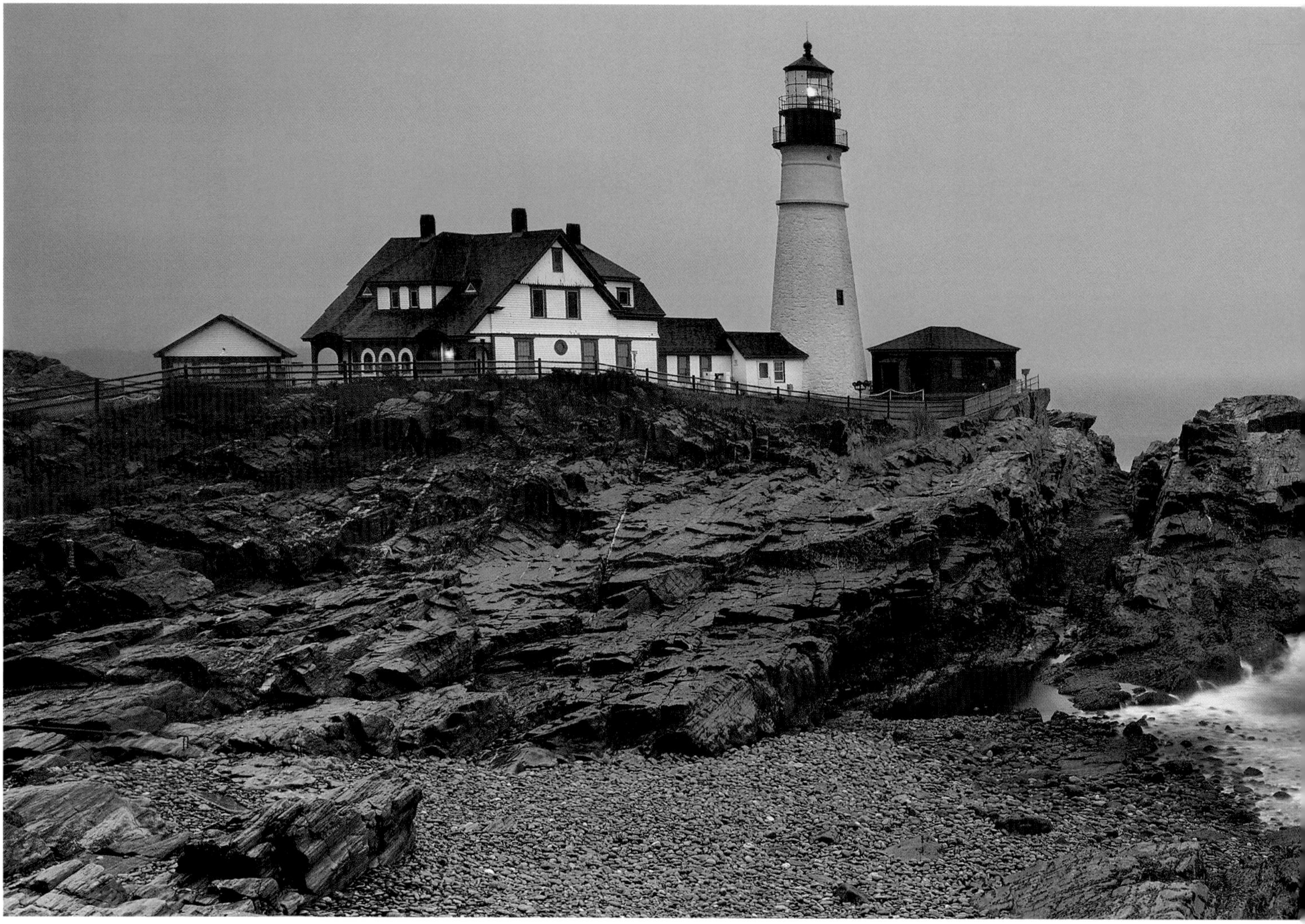

YOU ARE THE LIGHT OF THE WORLD.

A city that is set on a hill cannot be hidden.

Nor do they light a lamp and put it under a basket, but on a lampstand,

and it gives light to all who are in the house. Let your light so shine before men,

that they may see your good works and glorify your Father in heaven.

MATTHEW 6:14-16

Portland Head Lighthouse, Maine

Morality without religion is only a kind of dead reckoning—an endeavor to find our place on a cloudy sea by measuring the distance we have run, but without any observation of the heavenly bodies.

— *Henry Wadsworth Longfellow,* born 1807 in Portland, Maine

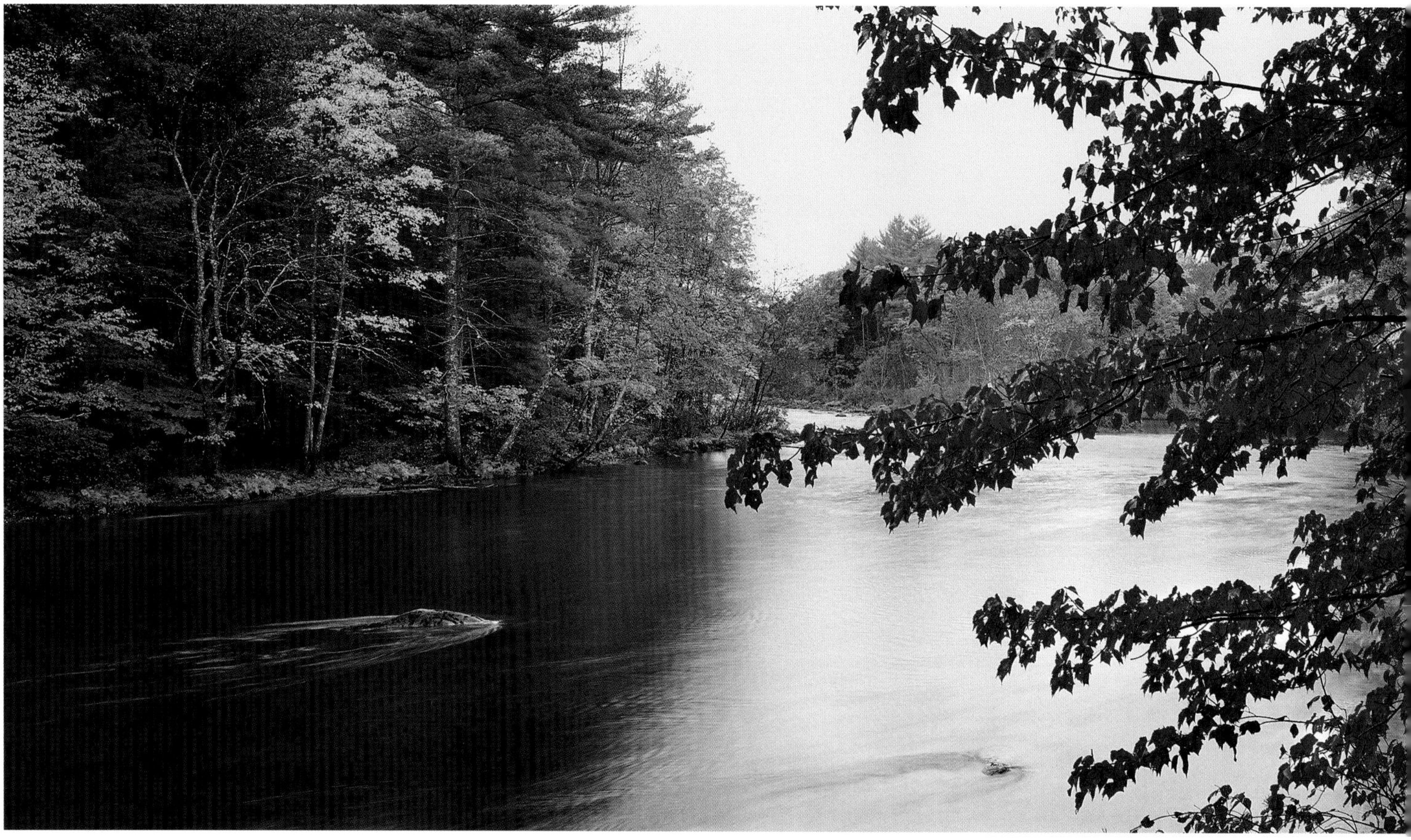

Ossipee River, Maine

The life of a man consists not in seeing visions and in dreaming dreams, but in active charity and in willing service.

— *Henry Wadsworth Longfellow*, born 1807 in Portland, Maine

I AM THE LORD YOUR GOD,

Who teaches you to profit,

Who leads you by the way you should go.

Oh, that you had heeded My commandments!

Then your peace would have been like a river,

And your righteousness like the waves of the sea.

ISAIAH 48:17-18

Maine

YOUR DESCENDANTS WILL INHERIT the nations,

And make the desolate cities inhabited.

Do not fear, for you will not be ashamed;

Neither be disgraced, for you will not be put to shame;

. . . Your Redeemer is the Holy One of Israel;

He is called the God of the whole earth.

ISAIAH 54:2-5

SPOCOTT WINDMILL, LLOYD, MARYLAND

I had reasoned this out in my mind, there was one of two things I had a right to, liberty or death; if I could not have one, I would have the other.

— *Harriet Tubman,* Abolitionist, Social Reformer
Born 1820 in Dorchester County, Maryland

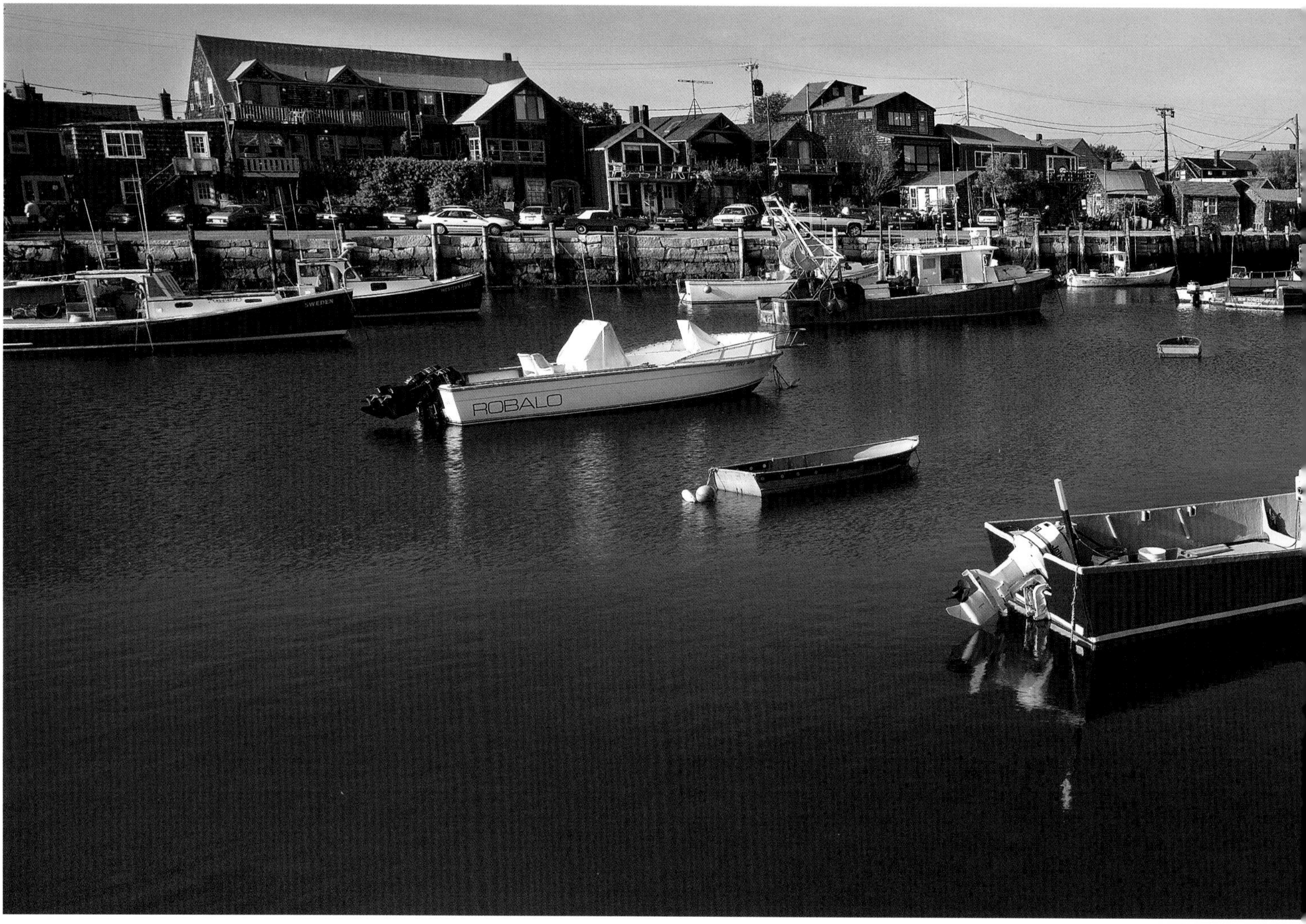

THIS HOPE we have as an anchor of the soul,

both sure and steadfast.

HEBREWS 6:19

Rockport, Massachusetts

To reach a port we must sail, sometimes with the wind, and sometimes against it. But we must not drift or lie at anchor.

— *Oliver Wendell Holmes,* Poet, Physician, Harvard Professor
Born 1809 in Cambridge, Massachusetts

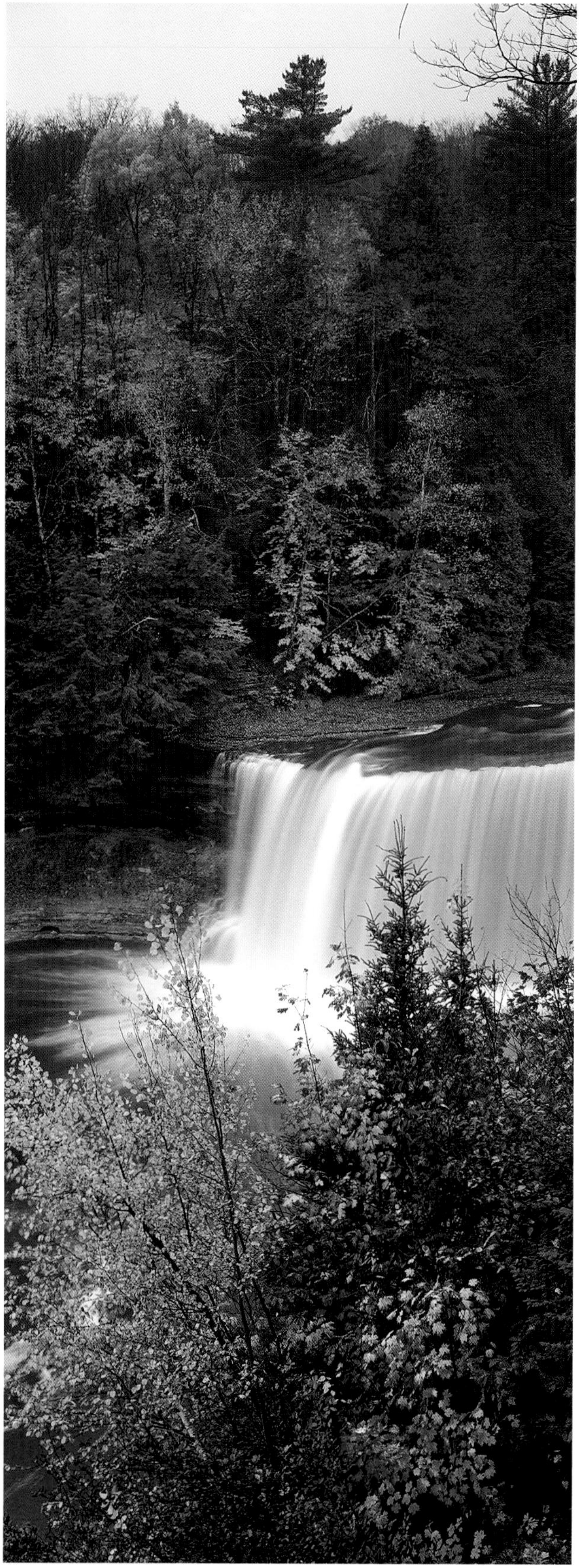

What's right about America is that although we have a mess of problems, we have great capacity—intellect and resources—to do something about them.

— *Henry Ford,* Industrialist,
Born 1863 in Dearborn, Michigan

UPPER TAHQUAMENON FALLS, MICHIGAN

MERCY AND TRUTH

have met together;

Righteousness and peace have kissed.

Truth shall spring out of the earth,

And righteousness shall look down from heaven.

Yes, the LORD will give what is good;

And our land will yield its increase.

PSALM 85:10-12

AS THE DEER PANTS for the water brooks,

So pants my soul for You, O God.

PSALM 42:1

LOWER TAHQUAMENON FALLS, MICHIGAN

This is the land of Longfellow's "Hiawatha." Long before the white man set eyes on this river, the abundance of fish in its waters and animals along its shores attracted the Ojibwa people who camped, farmed, fished, and trapped along its banks. The air is still charged with life and the thunderous roar of the falls clears any troubling thoughts. All is well and the river of life flows on.

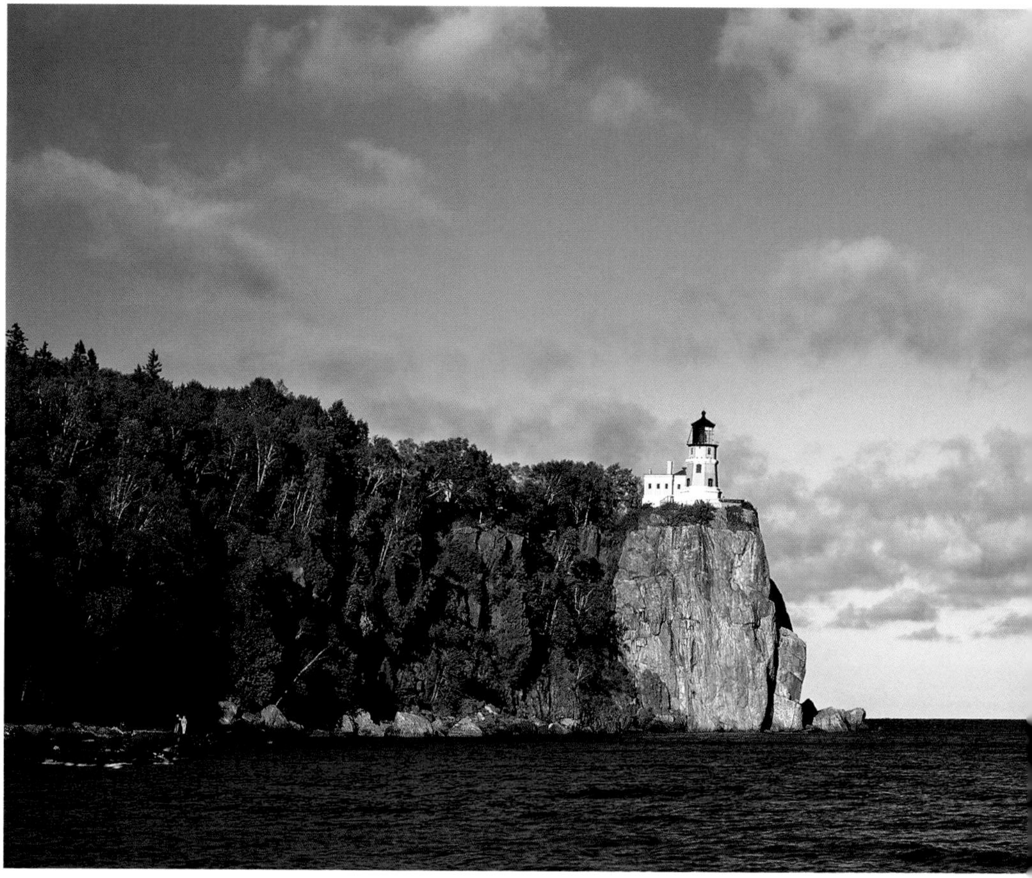

THEN GOD SAID,

"Let the waters under the heavens be gathered together into one place,

and let the dry land appear"; and it was so.

And God called the dry land Earth,

and the gathering together of the waters He called Seas.

And God saw that it was good.

GENESIS 1:9-10

Split Rock Lighthouse, Minnesota

A storm in November 1905 damaged twenty-nine ships, sinking two, off the Minnesota coast of Lake Superior. Soon afterward, work was begun on a lighthouse at Split Rock to help prevent another such calamity. God's Word is a lighthouse that warns us away from dangerous waters and directs us back to the safer channel. We don't have to wreck our lives, because He's given us all the help we need to endure life's storms.

I WILL HEAL their backsliding,

I will love them freely,

For My anger has turned away from him.

I will be like the dew to Israel;

He shall grow like the lily,

And lengthen his roots like Lebanon.

HOSEA 14:4-5

Lotus Flowers, Mississippi

Mississippi is a lush, verdant land blessed with great beauty. Much of the state's history is dominated by the seasonal changes of the mighty Mississippi River, America's Nile, which in some places is more than a mile wide. Even away from the river, numerous wetlands abound with life. Such is the wealth of America.

Delta Queen, Natchez, Mississippi

This gracious lady of the river helps sustain the romance of a bygone era. In the golden years from 1811 until the turn of the century, paddlewheel steamboats were directly responsible for accelerating the development of the American frontier. The *Delta Queen,* one of the few remaining authentic paddle steamers, is shown here moored for the evening before continuing her adventure up the grand old Mississippi. As Mark Twain once said, "The river is a wonderful book, with a new story to tell every day."

FEAR NOT, for I have redeemed you;

I have called you by your name;

You are Mine.

When you pass through the waters, I will be with you;

And through the rivers, they shall not overflow you.

ISAIAH 43:1-2

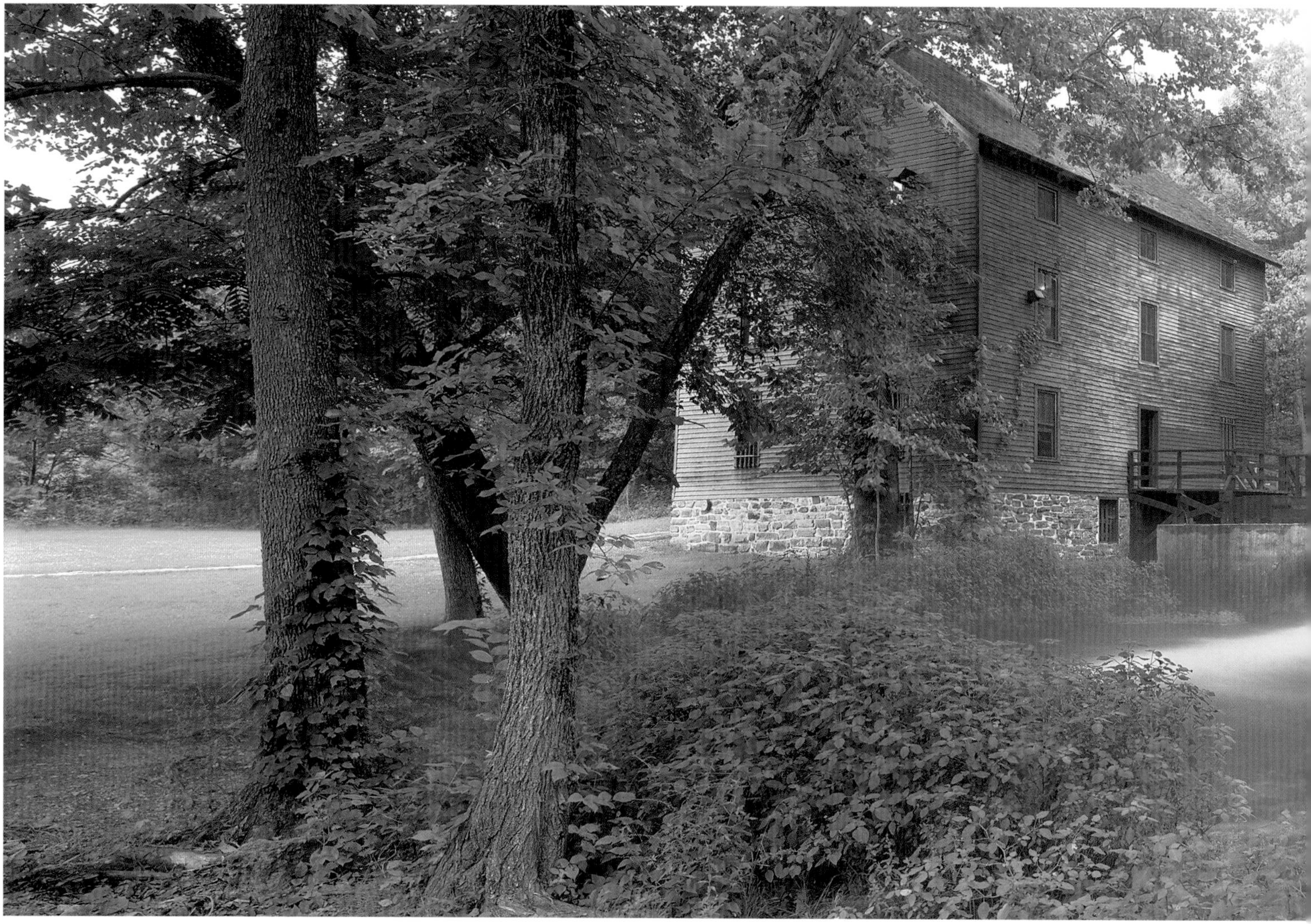

KEEP YOUR HEART with all diligence,

For out of it spring the issues of life.

PROVERBS 4:23

Alley Spring Mill, Missouri

This historic mill (built 1893-1894) once served the Alley Spring community as a place where people gathered to grind their wheat into flour. Nearby stood a small schoolhouse where local children could learn and that served as a church on Sundays. Around the springs were glider rockers where locals and tourists alike could relax and enjoy the rich beauty of their surroundings. Memories of these core facets of community—faith, friendship, commerce, and education—still echo above the burbling water.

WHO IS LIKE YOU, O LORD, among the gods?

Who is like You, glorious in holiness,

Fearful in praises, doing wonders?

EXODUS 15:11

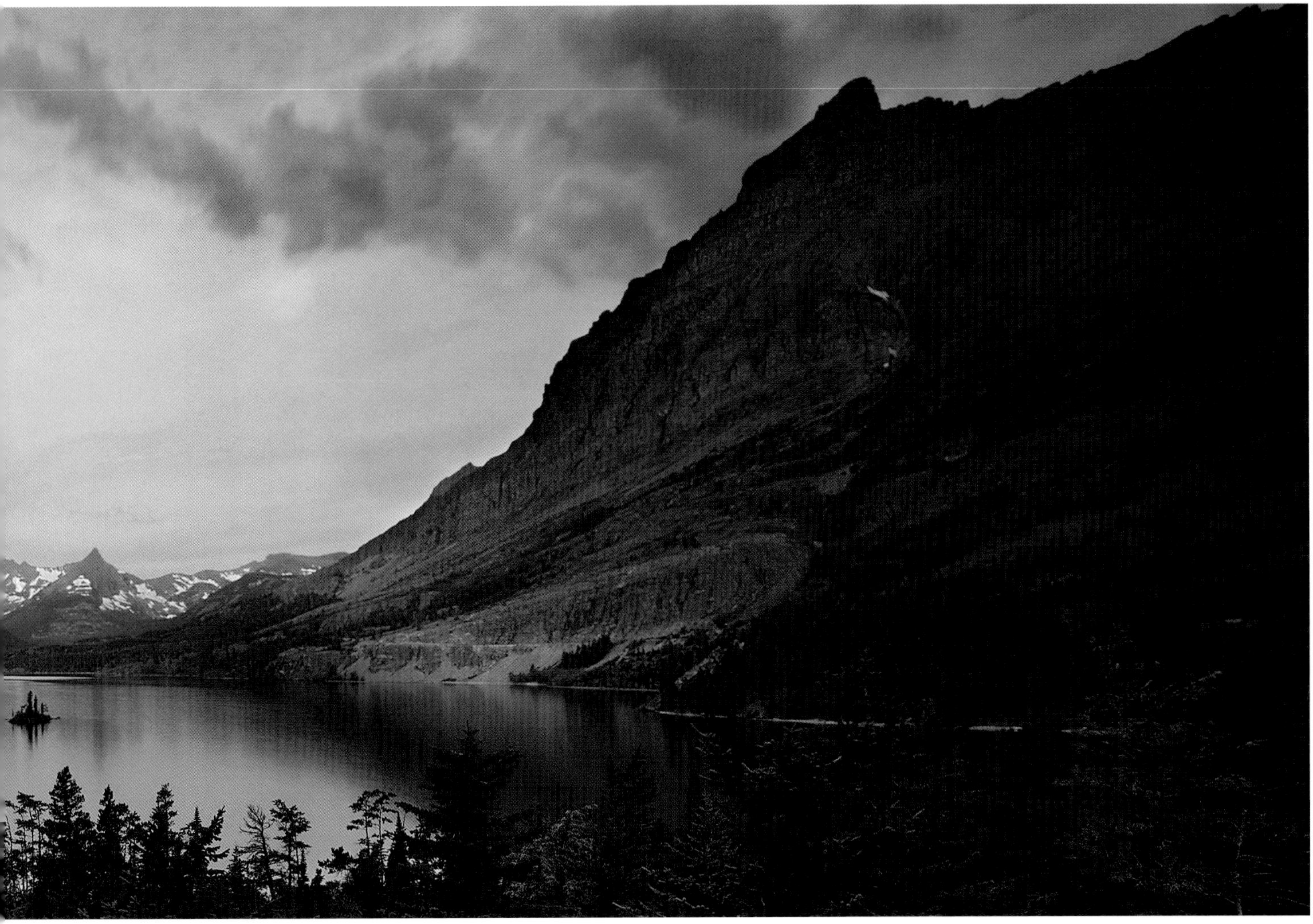

St. Mary Lake, Glacier National Park, Montana

Glacier National Park is one of the most pristine areas on earth, with hundreds of waterfalls and clear, cold lakes amid the mountain peaks. It is considered a world heritage site for its natural importance as a beautiful place to study an intact ecosystem. This park borders a similar one in Canada, and the two together are the world's first peace park, symbolizing friendship between the two nations.

The contrast between the ethereal pink light and the surrounding shadows gives this scene an incredible sense of otherworldly presence. I had been told that sunset was the best time to photograph this location, but I felt I should try for a sunrise shot. When I first arrived in the pre-dawn dark, all I could see was the craggy outline of the mountains, but as the sun began to touch the sky with light, God painted the clouds with a beautiful pink-apricot radiance.

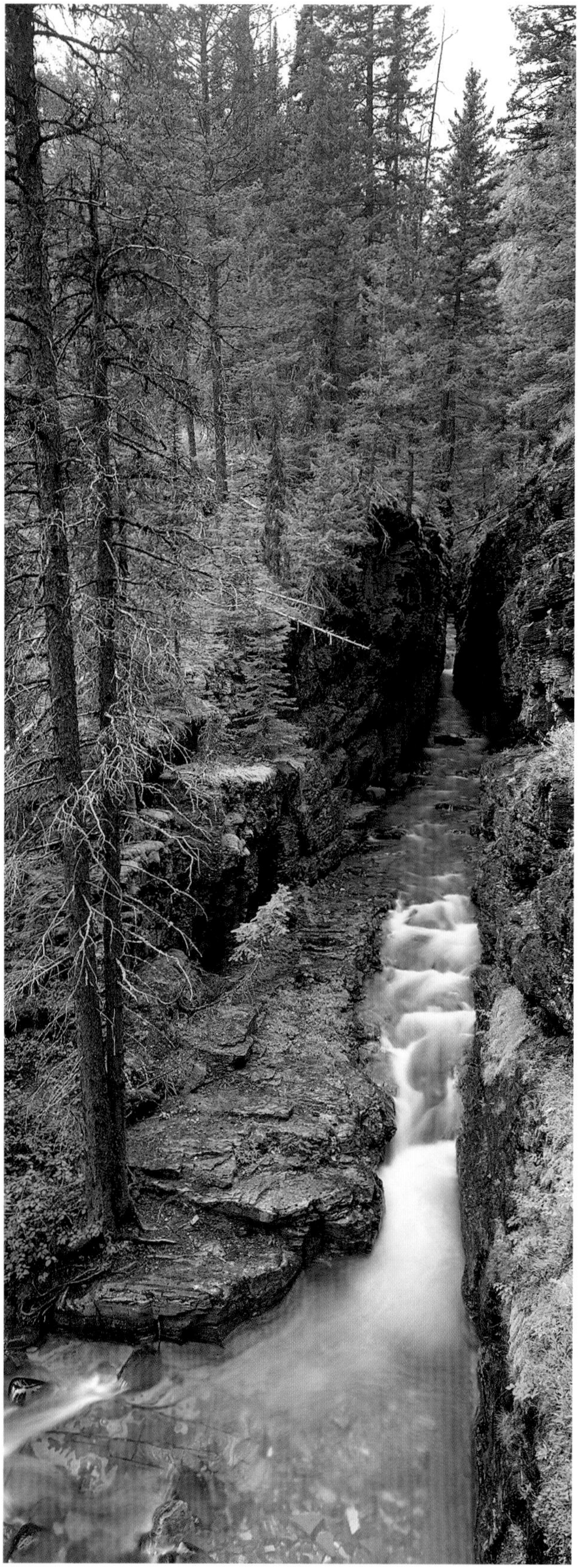

Baring Creek roars through the narrow channel of Sunrift Gorge near a series of breathtaking waterfalls.

Sundrift Gorge, Glacier National Park, Montana

ENTER BY THE NARROW GATE;

for wide is the gate and broad is the way

that leads to destruction,

and there are many who go in by it.

Because narrow is the gate and difficult is the way

which leads to life, and there are few who find it.

MATTHEW 7:13-14

HE WHO FORMS MOUNTAINS,

And creates the wind,

Who declares to man what his thought is,

And makes the morning darkness,

Who treads the high places of the earth—

The LORD God of hosts is His name.

AMOS 4:13

Seven Windmills, Watson Ranch, Nebraska

Feeding people is among the most basic of human needs, and much of America's wealth lies in its fertile breadbasket. The Watson Ranch contributed to that wealth by experimenting with alfalfa in the late 1800s. Farmers learned they could grow this crop not only to feed poultry but more importantly to make the soil more fertile. People around the world have more to eat today because of the American farmers who dared to try new things.

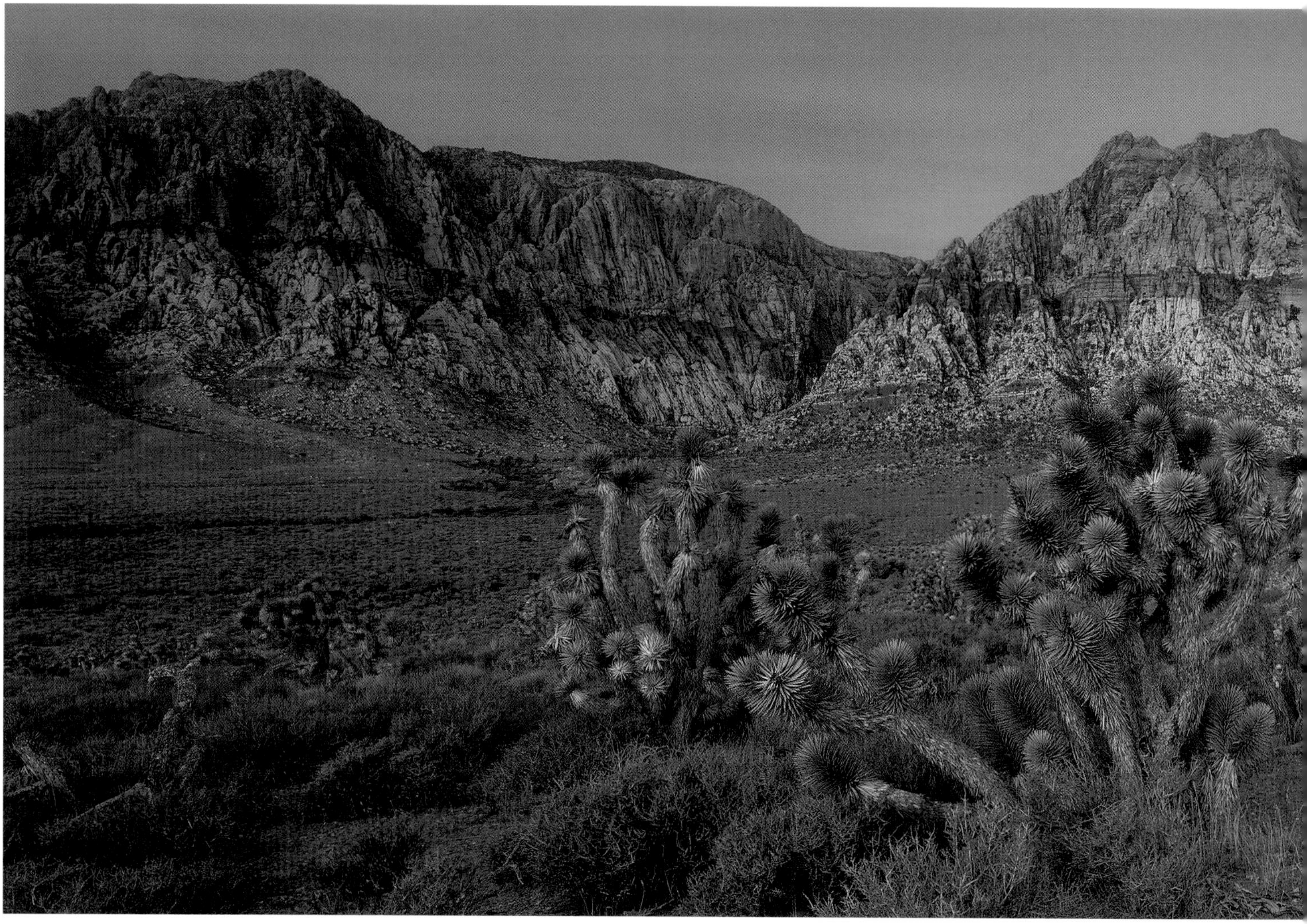

THE LORD YOUR GOD LED YOU

all the way these forty years in the wilderness, to humble you and test you,

to know what was in your heart, whether you would keep His commandments or not.

So He humbled you, allowed you to hunger, and fed you with manna

which you did not know nor did your fathers know,

that He might make you know that man shall not live by bread alone;

but man lives by every word that proceeds from the mouth of the LORD.

DEUTERONOMY 8:2-3

Desert near Red Rock Canyon, Nevada

When God freed His people from captivity in Egypt, He meant to free their hearts, not just their bodies, so He led them into the wilderness. Amid the starkness of the desert, their hearts were laid bare. They were completely dependent on God, and they learned to trust Him. Today, people still come to the simple places to contemplate their lives and find the oasis of God's benevolent truth.

BE STILL, AND KNOW THAT I AM GOD;

I will be exalted among the nations,

I will be exalted in the earth!

PSALM 46:10

Chocorua Lake, New Hampshire

The same God whose commandments keep us busy taking care of one another and preparing for His return is the same God who also tells us to simply "Be still." We all need times of stillness, peace, tranquility. We need time to float. Time to bask in the wonder of our God and all that He has made and done.

PUT ON TENDER MERCIES,

kindness, humility, meekness, longsuffering; bearing with one another,

and forgiving one another, if anyone has a complaint against another;

even as Christ forgave you, so you also must do.

But above all these things put on love, which is the bond of perfection.

And let the peace of God rule in your hearts,

to which also you were called in one body; and be thankful.

COLOSSIANS 3:12-15

Waterloo Covered Bridge, Warner, New Hampshire

A bridge is a wonderful thing. It connects two places that otherwise would stay apart, and thereby it connects the people who otherwise would have difficulty meeting to share knowledge, experiences, and resources. America is a land rich with bridges—between cultures, between socioeconomic classes, between disparate ideas. Even more significant than the ideological bridges, though, is the span God bridged between heaven and earth by sending Jesus. Now all who believe are called on to continue building bridges that help lead people to the Lord.

Pittstown, New Jersey

The home is a sacred place. This is where we feel safest and most ourselves. This is where we raise our children and teach them the essentials of life. This is where our thoughts turn when we're ill, or sad, or lonely. At home, our friends and family can unburden their hearts and find comfort in the beauty of simply being together. The United States was built on homes where faith and hope prevailed. May it ever be so!

FOR I KNOW THE THOUGHTS that I think toward you, says the LORD, thoughts of peace and not of evil, to give you a future and a hope. Then you will call upon Me and go and pray to Me, and I will listen to you. And you will seek Me and find Me, when you search for Me with all your heart.

JEREMIAH 29:11-13

New Jersey

WHO AMONG YOU FEARS THE LORD?

Who obeys the voice of His Servant?

Who walks in darkness

And has no light?

Let him trust in the name of the LORD

And rely upon his God.

ISAIAH 50:10

White Sands National Monument, New Mexico

The huge white sand dunes of New Mexico are breathtaking. This particular shot was taken at sunrise, so we needed to find the location in the dark. The previous day we had marked the area with a GPS, and in the dark of the early morning it took us an hour to reach this remote site. While walking in total darkness I stared intently at the GPS screen for navigation, trusting it for guidance. When the dawn light finally came we were happy to confirm we were in the right place. I spent several moments being amazed at the technology behind the GPS. We trusted signals from satellites out in space. We couldn't see the satellites or the signals, but we trusted in them and we found our mark. That's just like God—if we trust in Him, even in the darkness He will guide us to where we need to be. He wants to walk with us and be our personal GPS (God Positioning System), but we have to trust Him and walk in His way.

American Falls, Niagara Falls, New York

Niagara Falls is synonymous with power. No one can visit the falls and leave unaffected by their grandeur. Although there are higher waterfalls in the country, Niagara is the most powerful, with an average of four million cubic feet of water roaring down every minute, every day, for thousands of years. When you start to feel discouraged, just look to Niagara and remind yourself that God pours out His blessings with even more power.

BEHOLD, THE GLORY of the God of Israel

came from the way of the east.

His voice was like the sound of many waters;

and the earth shone with His glory.

EZEKIEL 43:2

New York

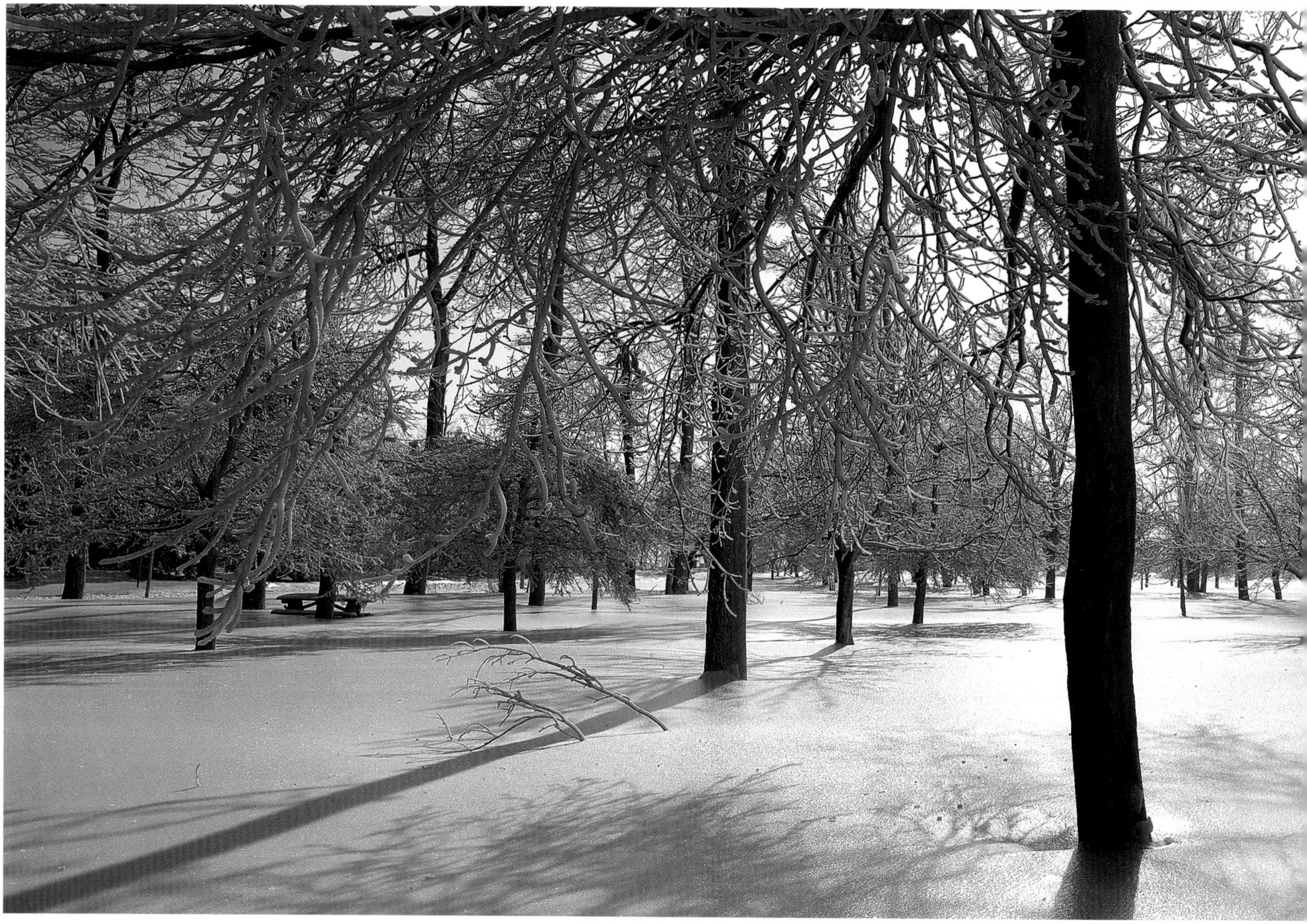

WASH ME, and I shall be whiter than snow.

Make me hear joy and gladness . . .

Hide Your face from my sins,

And blot out all my iniquities.

Create in me a clean heart, O God,

And renew a steadfast spirit within me.

PSALM 51:7-10

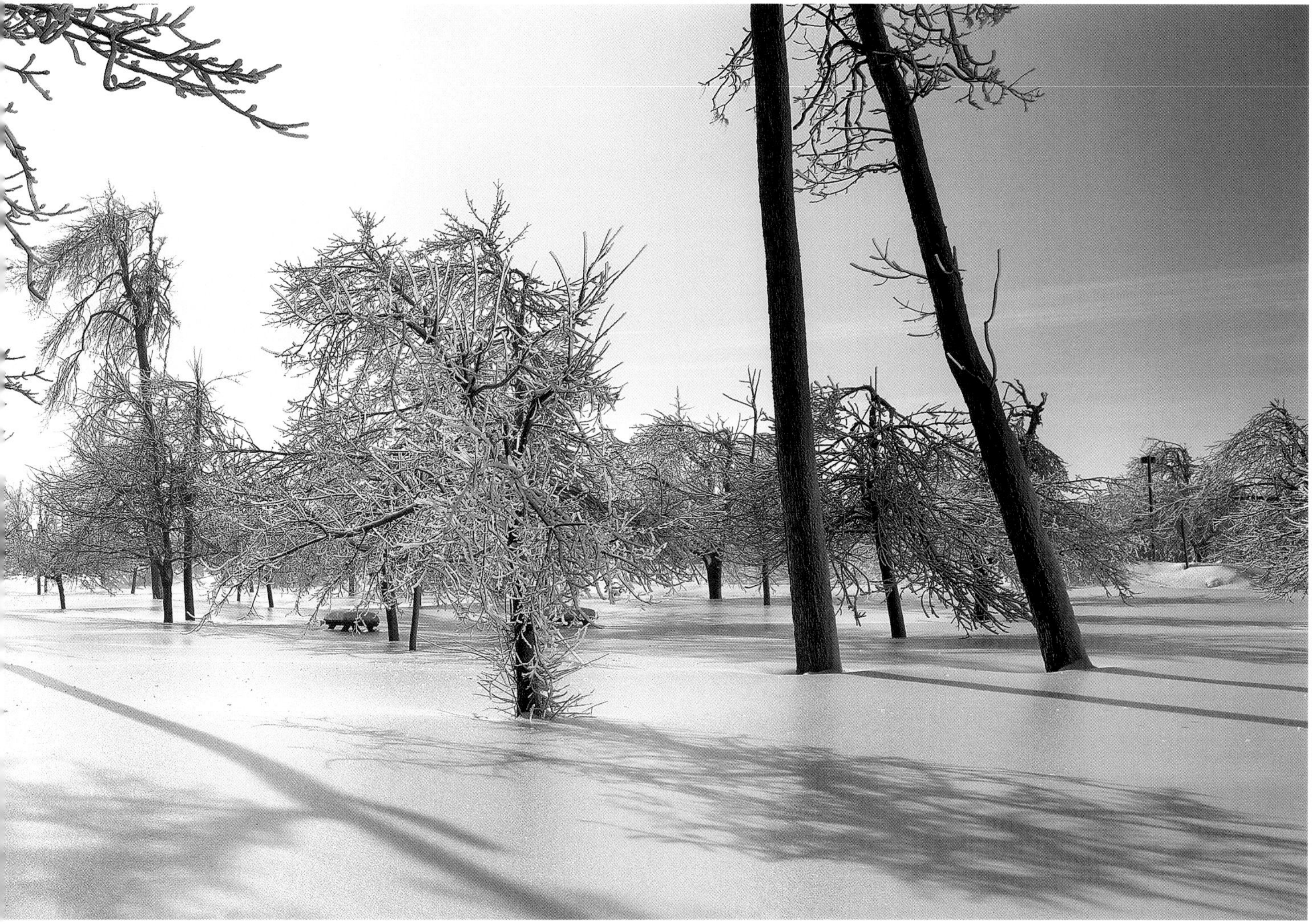

Frozen Park, Niagara Falls, New York

Winter is part of life. The things of the earth have to die in order to grow again to greater life. When the winter places of your heart lie cold and still, find comfort in the spring just around the corner.

I WILL PRAISE YOU, O Lord, among the peoples;

I will sing to You among the nations.

For Your mercy reaches unto the heavens,

And Your truth unto the clouds.

Be exalted, O God, above the heavens;

Let Your glory be above all the earth.

PSALM 57:9-11

Blue Ridge Parkway, North Carolina

The Blue Ridge Parkway is a great feat of American perseverance and ingenuity as it runs along the scenic Appalachians and passes through twenty-seven tunnels. It took fifty-two years to complete. But God always puts the greatness of human accomplishment into perspective. When the clouds settle just below the peaks and the sun lends fiery color to the autumn leaves, there's no mistaking the immensity of the One who made it all.

I WILL POUR WATER on him who is thirsty,

And floods on the dry ground;

I will pour My Spirit on your descendants,

And My blessing on your offspring.

ISAIAH 44:1

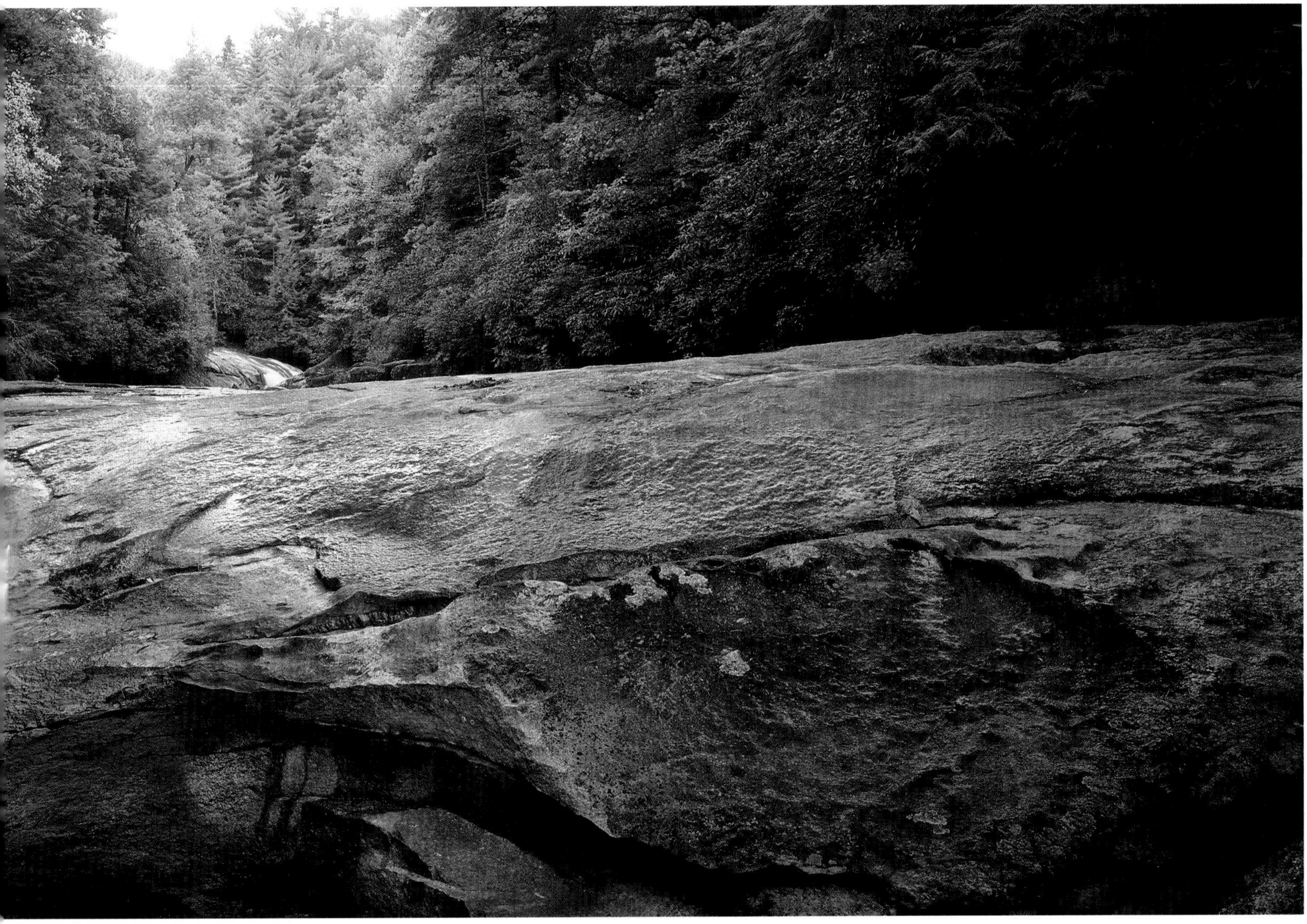

Horsepasture River, Nantahala National Forest, North Carolina

No people ought to feel greater obligations to celebrate the goodness of the Great Disposer of events and the Destiny of Nations than the people of the United States...And to the same Divine Author of every good and perfect gift we are indebted for all those privileges and advantages, religious as well as civil, which are so richly enjoyed in this favored land.

—*James Madison* U. S. President (1809-1817), Father of the Constitution

BE STRONG and of good courage;

do not be afraid, nor be dismayed,

for the LORD your God is with you wherever you go.

JOSHUA 1:9

Maltese Cabin, Medora, North Dakota

Thrice happy is the nation that has a glorious history. Far better it is to dare mighty things, to win glorious triumphs, even though checkered by failure, than to take rank with those poor spirits who neither enjoy much nor suffer much, because they live in the gray twilight that knows neither victory nor defeat.

— *Theodore Roosevelt,* U.S. President (1901-1909)
Elkhorn Ranch, Medora, North Dakota

HE IS THE LORD our God;

His judgments are in all the earth.

Remember His covenant forever,

The word which He commanded, for a thousand generations.

I CHRONICLES 16:14-15

Old Ford Truck, Amidon, North Dakota

I love adventuring with God, and this shot came from one of those wonderful times. I was looking for something that would give dimension to the vast flat lands of North Dakota. I asked the property owner if it would be all right to photograph the old truck, and he seemed surprised by my interest. So he told me the story of the truck. His father had parked the pickup beside the barn many years earlier, and soon after that became ill and died. In memory of him the family just left it alone and there it still sits—Dad's Truck.

YOUR WORD is a lamp to my feet

And a light to my path.

PSALM 119:105

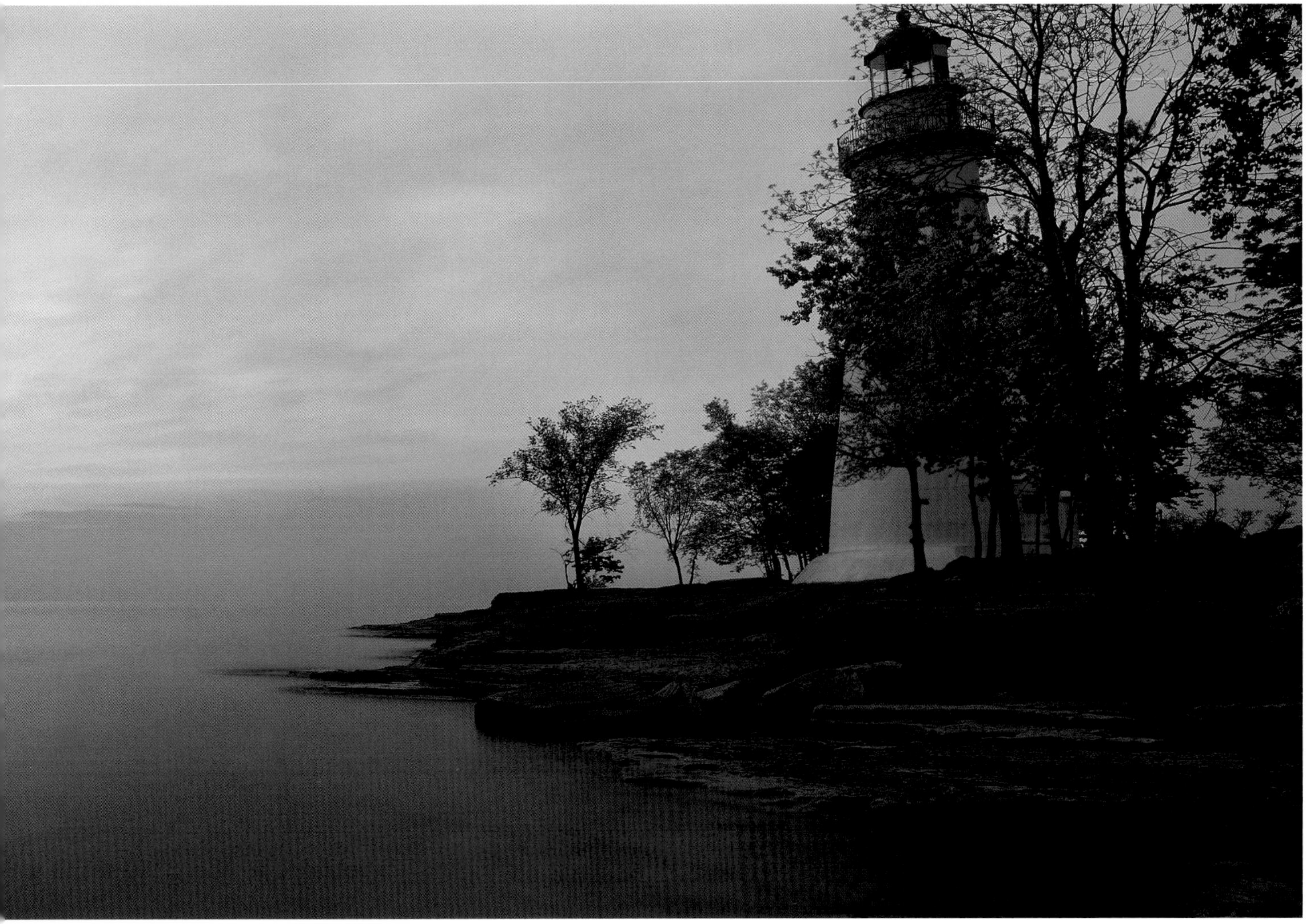

Marblehead Lighthouse, Lake Erie, Ohio

Marblehead Lighthouse has guarded the shore of Lake Erie since 1821, giving light to countless sailors. Although the technology of the tower has changed many times over the years, its mission has endured—it still lights the way. Similarly, the methods of America may change over the years, but the nation's vision of freedom and opportunity still shines for the whole world to see.

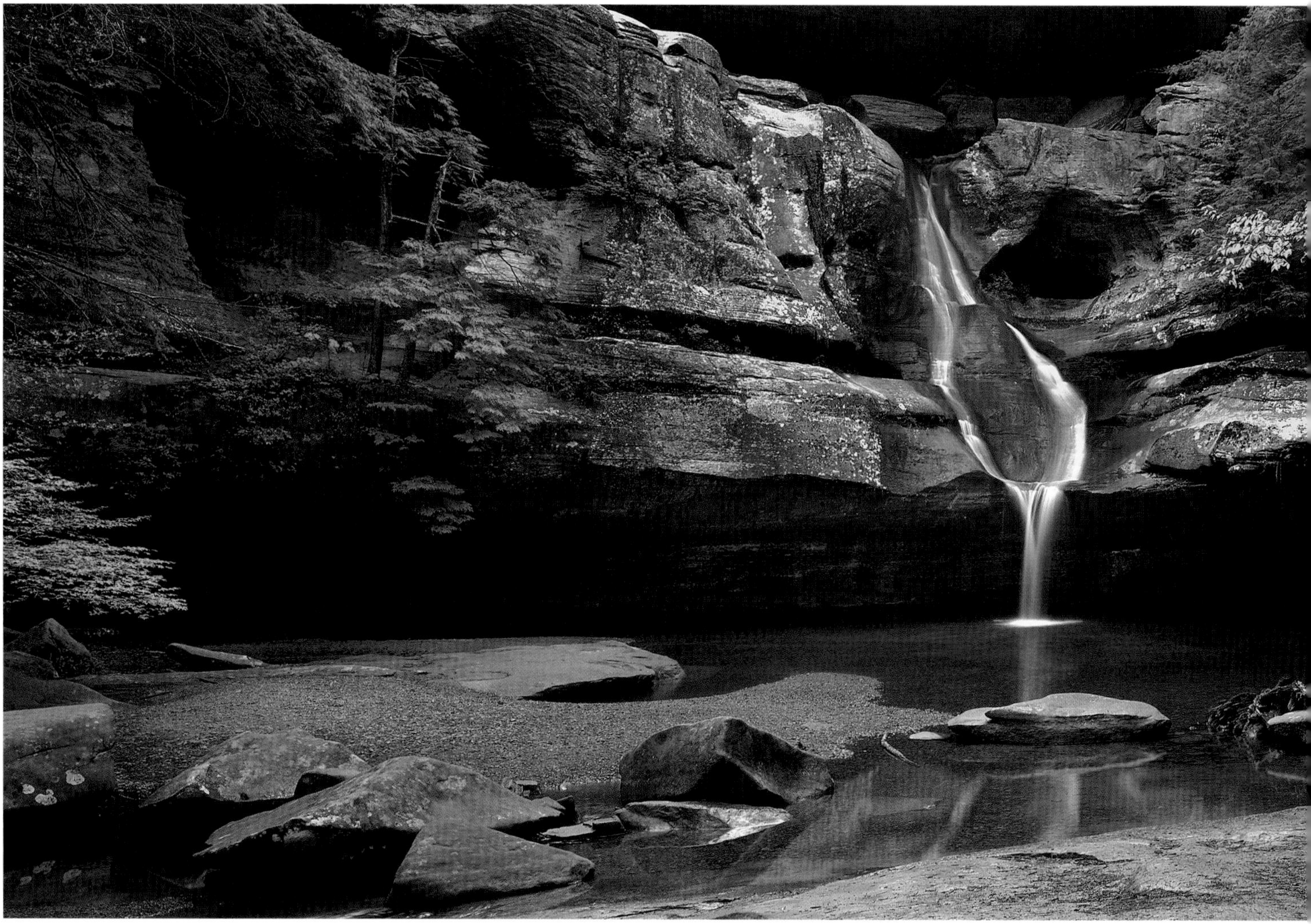

I EXHORT FIRST OF ALL that supplications,

prayers, intercessions, and giving of thanks be made for all men,

for kings and all who are in authority, that we may lead a quiet and peaceable

life in all godliness and reverence.

For this is good and acceptable in the sight of God our Savior.

1 TIMOTHY 2:1-3

Cedar Falls, Hocking Hills State Park, Ohio

In the Hocking Hills region of Ohio, one can almost imagine the frontier days of trappers, trailblazers, and brave families who pushed west through the wilderness to create new homes. Before settling in the farmland of the Ohio Valley, they had to pass through the Appalachians with all the danger and incredible beauty God poured out on this land.

Scudder School, Prairie Song, Oklahoma

Freedom means little unless you know how to use it well. That's why education is a cornerstone of American life. The world's first public schools started in Colonial America, and the emphasis continued as frontier communities established one-room schoolhouses as soon as possible.

Promote then, as an object of primary importance, institutions for the general diffusion of knowledge. In proportion as the structure of a government gives force to public opinion, it is essential that public opinion should be enlightened.

—*George Washington, U. S. President (1789-1797)*

TRAIN UP A CHILD in the way he should go,

And when he is old he will not depart from it. . . .

The eyes of the LORD preserve knowledge,

But He overthrows the words of the faithless.

PROVERBS 22:6, 12

Oklahoma

O MY GOD, my soul is cast down within me;

Therefore I will remember You. . . .

Deep calls unto deep at the noise of Your waterfalls;

All Your waves and billows have gone over me.

The LORD will command

His lovingkindness in the daytime,

And in the night His song shall be with me—

A prayer to the God of my life.

PSALM 42:6-8

Oregon

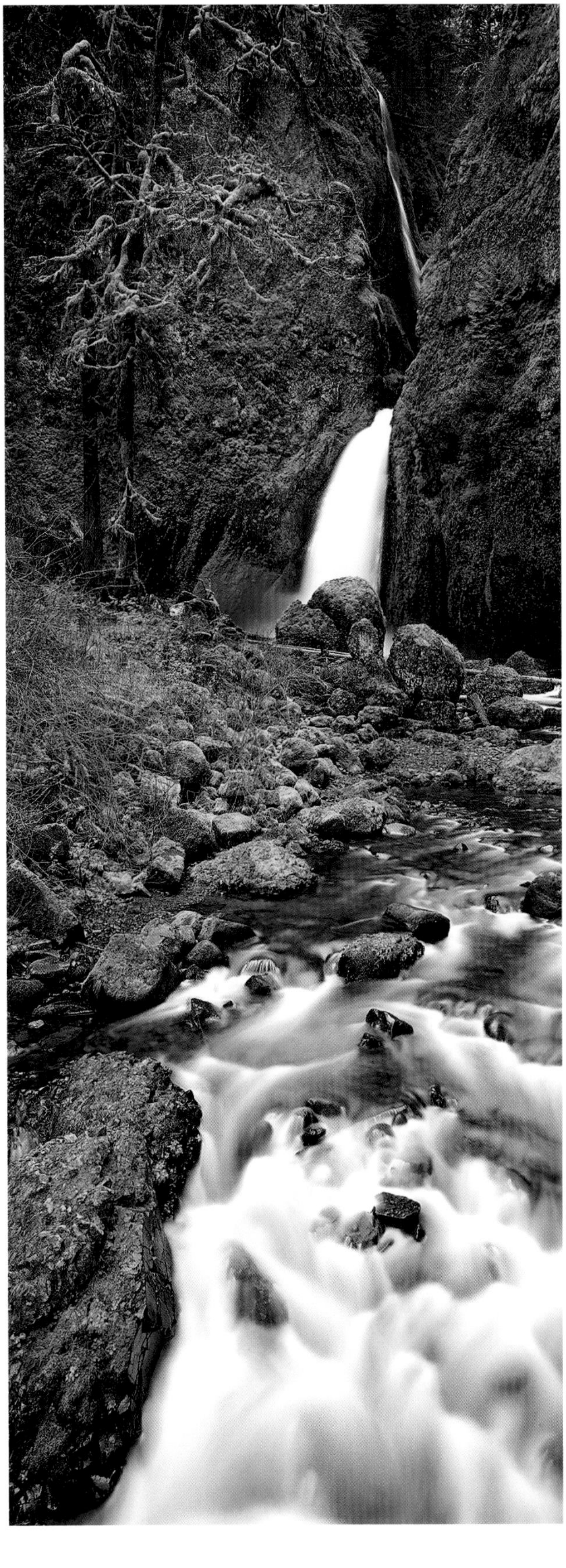

The top of Wahclella Falls hides among the basalt crannies of the Columbia River Gorge before it emerges to plunge into a pool at its base. Many powerful, amazing things start from secret sources. No one may know all the good things you do quietly every day, but someday their result will pour forth in glory.

Wahclella Falls, Columbia River Wilderness, Oregon

Lancaster, Pennsylvania

Religious freedom is one of America's core tenets, and William Penn was especially instrumental in establishing that precedent as founder of Pennsylvania in 1681. Many of his views on freedoms and democratic government were integrated into the development of the current U.S. Constitution. In the 18th and 19th centuries, the Amish immigrated from Germany to Lancaster County, where they still enjoy the freedoms guaranteed by this early vision of America as a haven for tolerance.

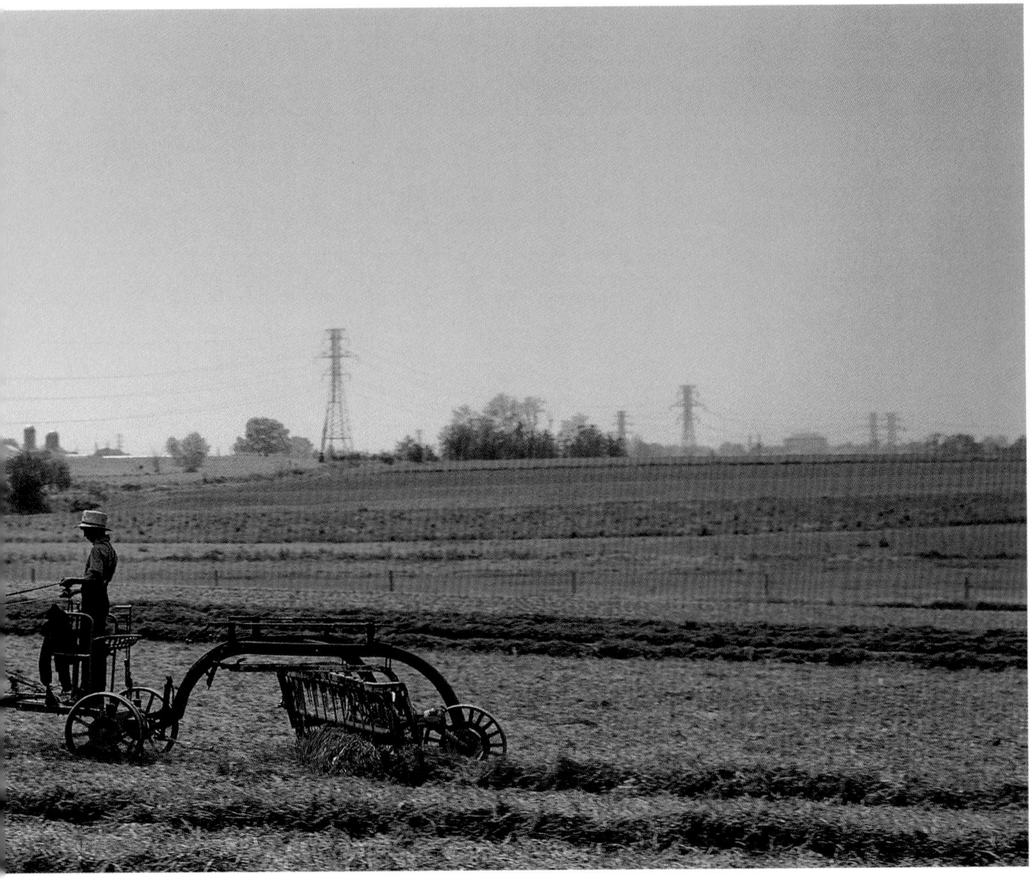

SOW FOR YOURSELVES RIGHTEOUSNESS;

Reap in mercy;

Break up your fallow ground,

For it is time to seek the LORD,

Till He comes and rains righteousness on you.

HOSEA 10:12

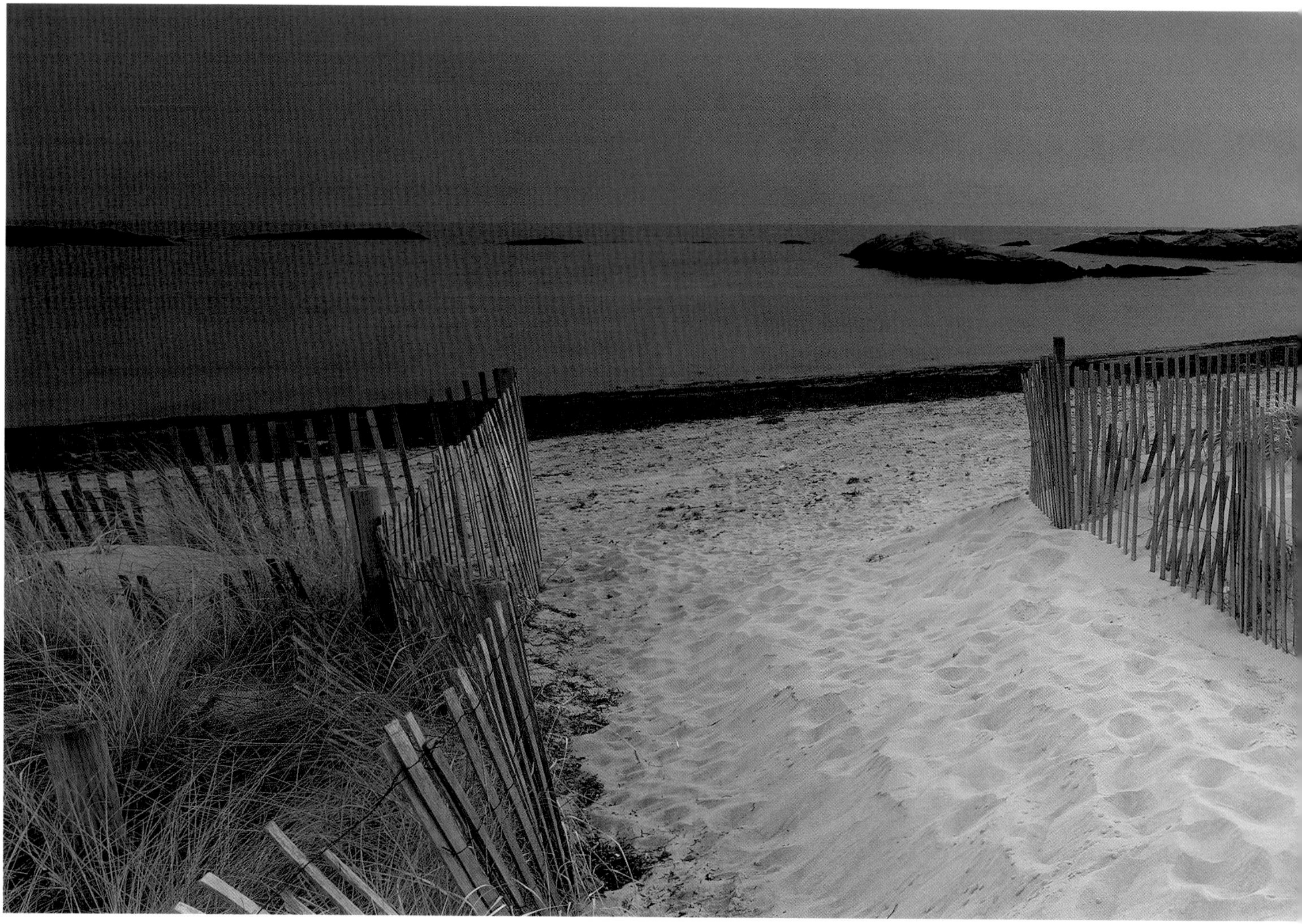

I WILL BLESS YOU,

and multiplying I will multiply your descendants

as the stars of the heaven and as the sand which is on the seashore;

and your descendants shall possess the gate of their enemies.

In your seed all the nations of the earth shall be blessed,

because you have obeyed My voice.

GENESIS 22:17-18

GOOSEBERRY BEACH, NEWPORT, RHODE ISLAND

Generations of families have grown up sailing, fishing, splashing, and chasing hermit crabs along the many beaches of New England.

THE EARTH IS THE LORD'S,

and all its fullness, the world and those who dwell therein.

PSALM 24:1

Hunting Island State Park, South Carolina

The semi-tropical vegetation of Hunting Island State Park does its best to resist the relentlessly encroaching seas at North Beach. The more firmly rooted the trees are, the longer they will stand.

RIGHTEOUSNESS EXALTS A NATION,

but sin is a disgrace to any people.

PSALM 14:34

Mount Rushmore, South Dakota

Four of America's most influential presidents—Washington, Jefferson, Roosevelt, and Lincoln—are immortalized as eternal watchmen over the land they once served. The grandeur of this monument is hard to appreciate until you stand in its presence, dwarfed by its magnitude, and ponder the mighty accomplishments of these giants of history.

Great Smoky Mountains, Tennessee

Providence has showered on this favored land blessings without number, and has chosen you as the guardians of freedom, to preserve it for the benefit of the human race. May He who holds in His hands the destinies of nations make you worthy of the favors He has bestowed and enable you, with pure hearts and pure hands and sleepless vigilance, to guard and defend to the end of time the great charge He has committed to your keeping.

—*Andrew Jackson,* U. S. President (1829-1837)
Hometown: Nashville, Tennessee

YOUR MERCY, O LORD, IS IN THE HEAVENS

Your faithfulness reaches to the clouds.

Your righteousness is like the great mountains;

Your judgments are a great deep;

O LORD, You preserve man and beast.

PSALM 36:5-6

Tennessee

HEAR, O ISRAEL: The LORD our God, the LORD is one!

You shall love the LORD your God with all your heart, with all your soul, and with all your strength.

And these words which I command you today shall be in your heart.

You shall teach them diligently to your children, and shall talk of them when you sit in your house,

when you walk by the way, when you lie down, and when you rise up.

You shall bind them as a sign on your hand, and they shall be as frontlets between your eyes.

You shall write them on the doorposts of your house and on your gates.

DEUTERONOMY 6:4-9

Carter Shields Cabin, Great Smoky Mountains National Park, Tennessee

Well may the boldest fear and the wisest tremble when incurring responsibilities on which may depend our country's peace and prosperity, and in some degree the hopes and happiness of the whole human family.

—*James K. Polk,* U. S. President (1845-1849)
Hometown: Columbia, Tennessee

THANKS BE TO GOD who always leads us in triumph in Christ,

and through us diffuses the fragrance of His knowledge in every place.

for we are to God the fragrance of Christ

among those who are being saved and among those who are perishing.

2 CORINTHIANS 2:14-15

Wildflowers, Texas

Under this covenant of justice, liberty, and union we have become a nation—prosperous, great, and mighty. And we have kept our freedom. But we have no promise from God that our greatness will endure. We have been allowed by Him to seek greatness with the sweat of our hands and the strength of our spirit. In each generation, with toil and tears, we have had to earn our heritage again. If we fail now then we will have forgotten in abundance what we learned in hardship; that democracy rests on faith, that freedom asks more than it gives, and the judgment of God is harshest on those who are most favored.

— *Lyndon B. Johnson,* U.S. President (1963-1969)

Born 1908 in Stonewall, Texas

AS IN WATER face reflects face,

So a man's heart reveals the man.

PROVERBS 27:19

Salt Flat, Guadalupe Mountains, Texas

This reflected image of mountains in a flooded salt flat seemed to come out of nowhere. Passing storms had dumped rain across this whole area of the Guadalupe Mountains. When I arrived here it was blowing a gale, and there were no reflections at all. I felt I should wait. By chance, there was a fallen sign beside the road, and we dragged it onto the sinking mud and used it as a platform. (From the road it must have looked as though I was standing on water!) I waited for hours on that little platform, buffeted by the wind. Finally, the clouds scattered across the scene into this letter "X" formation, the light broke through, and the wind stopped. It was a gift I could attribute only to the hand of God as I captured this vibrant pattern of mirrored rock and sky.

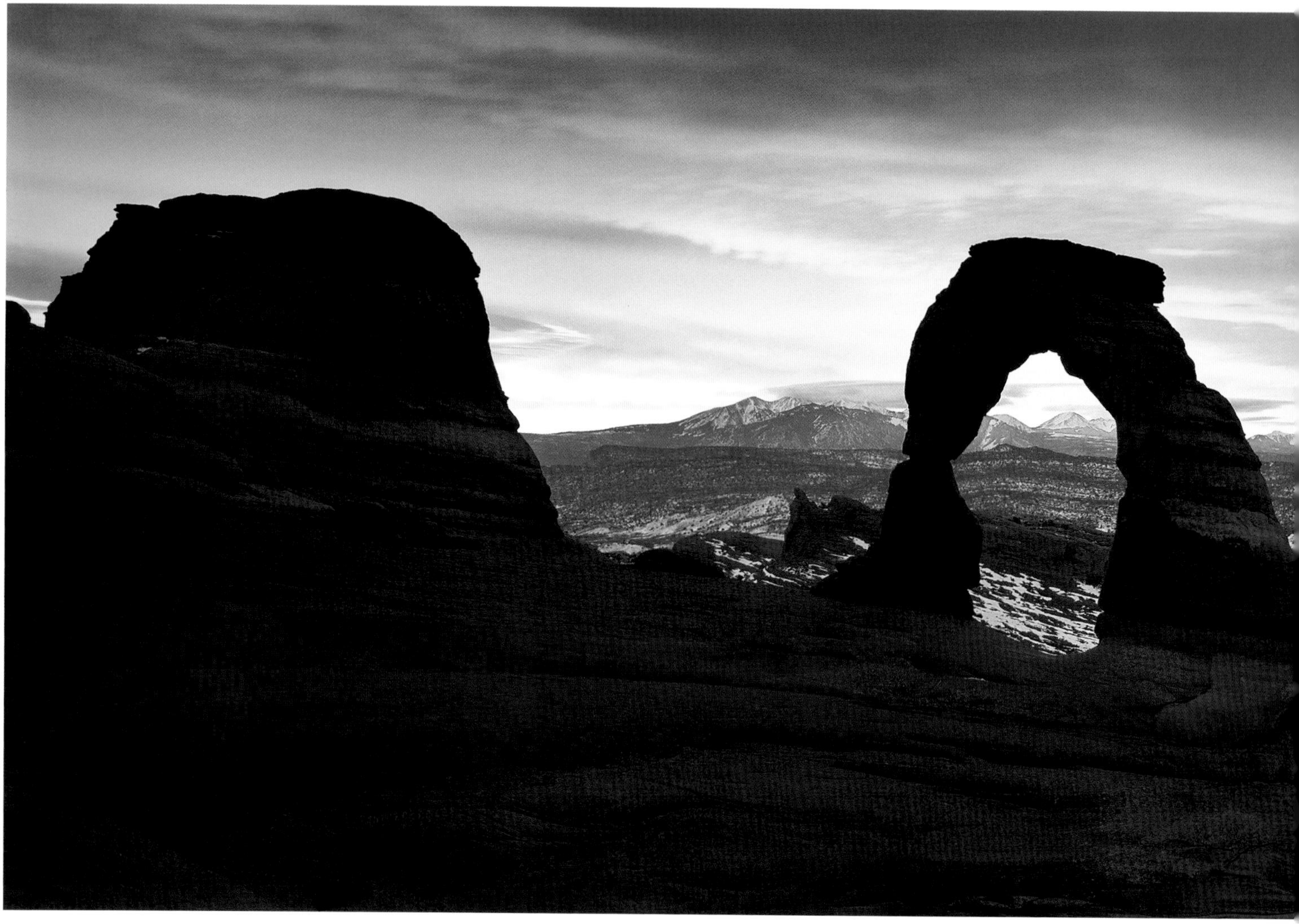

COMMIT YOUR WAY TO THE LORD,

Trust also in Him,

And He shall bring it to pass.

He shall bring forth your righteousness as the light,

And your justice as the noonday.

Rest in the LORD, and wait patiently for Him.

PSALM 37:5-7

SUNRISE AT DELICATE ARCH, UTAH

I came to this area with a guide who was very much into the New Age movement. I could see he was generally trying to search for truth, so I started sharing with him about the reality of Jesus. We became so engrossed in our conversation as we waited for the sun to rise that I inadvertently put on the wrong viewfinder—one meant for a much closer shot. The sun finally rose in a spectacular display of God's glory, and not until the moment was over and the light became bland did I realize the mistake I had made. I felt sick that I had blown a magnificent sunrise. Then I thought of the promise that "all things work together for good to those who love God, to those who are called according to His purpose" (Romans 8:28). So I prayed, "God, You know my heart. I was so consumed with telling the guide about You that I forgot about the photo, so the composition of this shot will be up to You." This is the shot He gave me, and He did a far better job than I could have done.

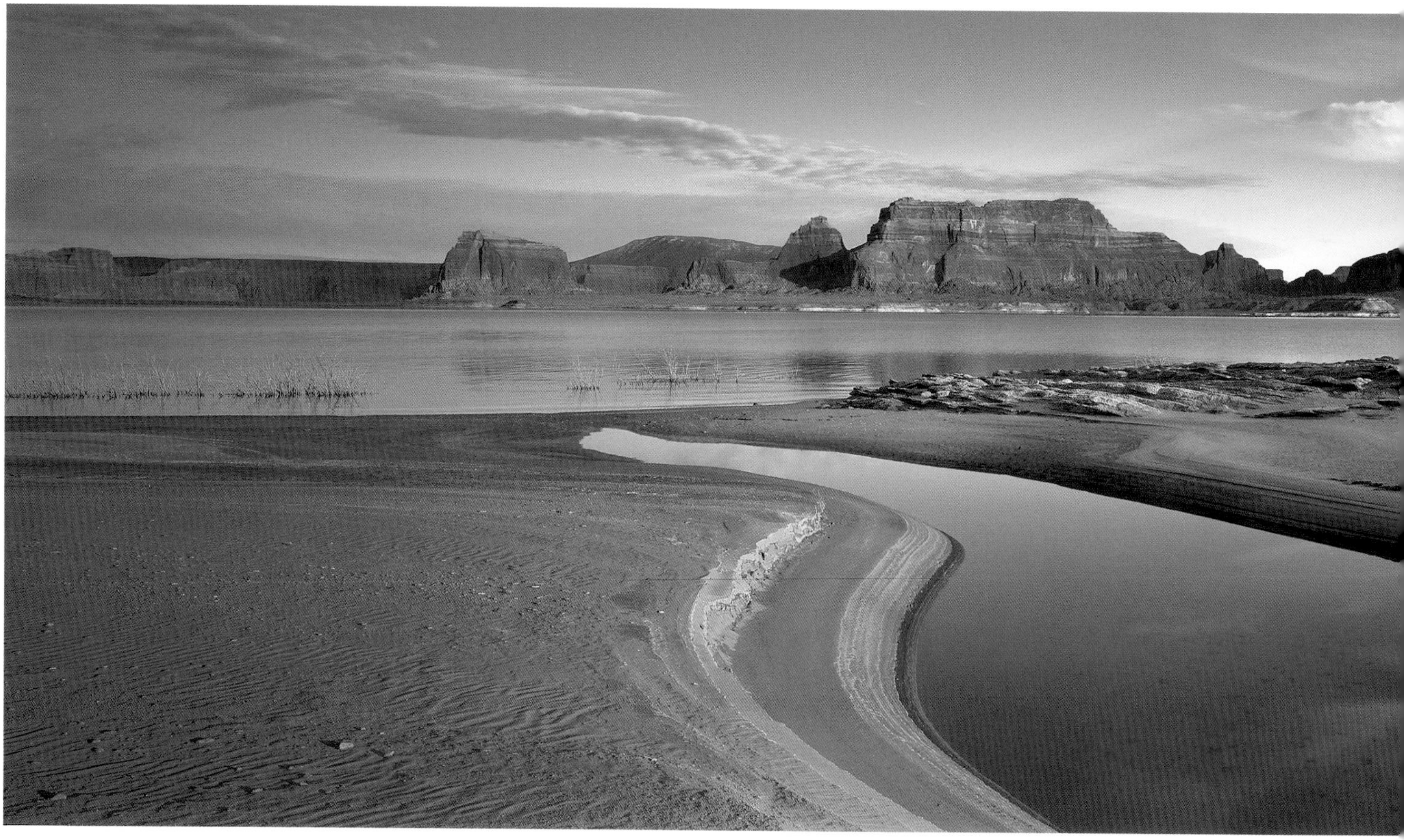

Padre Bay, Lake Powell, Utah

Lake Powell is one of the largest man-made reservoirs in the United States. It fills more than ninety canyons along the Colorado River, and it serves as a vital water source for Colorado, Utah, Wyoming, and New Mexico. It is also very popular as a recreation area. But the glory of the lake does not belong to the engineers who built it or the explorer for whom it's named; it belongs to the God who generously provided the geology, resources, and know-how for humans to adapt His creation as we see fit. He easily could thwart every change we attempt to His world, but instead He gives us the ability and freedom to choose for ourselves what we want to do with the planet. Thank You, God, for Your benevolence!

I GIVE WATERS IN THE WILDERNESS

And rivers in the desert,

To give drink to My people, My chosen.

This people I have formed for Myself;

They shall declare My praise.

ISAIAH 43:20–21

Utah

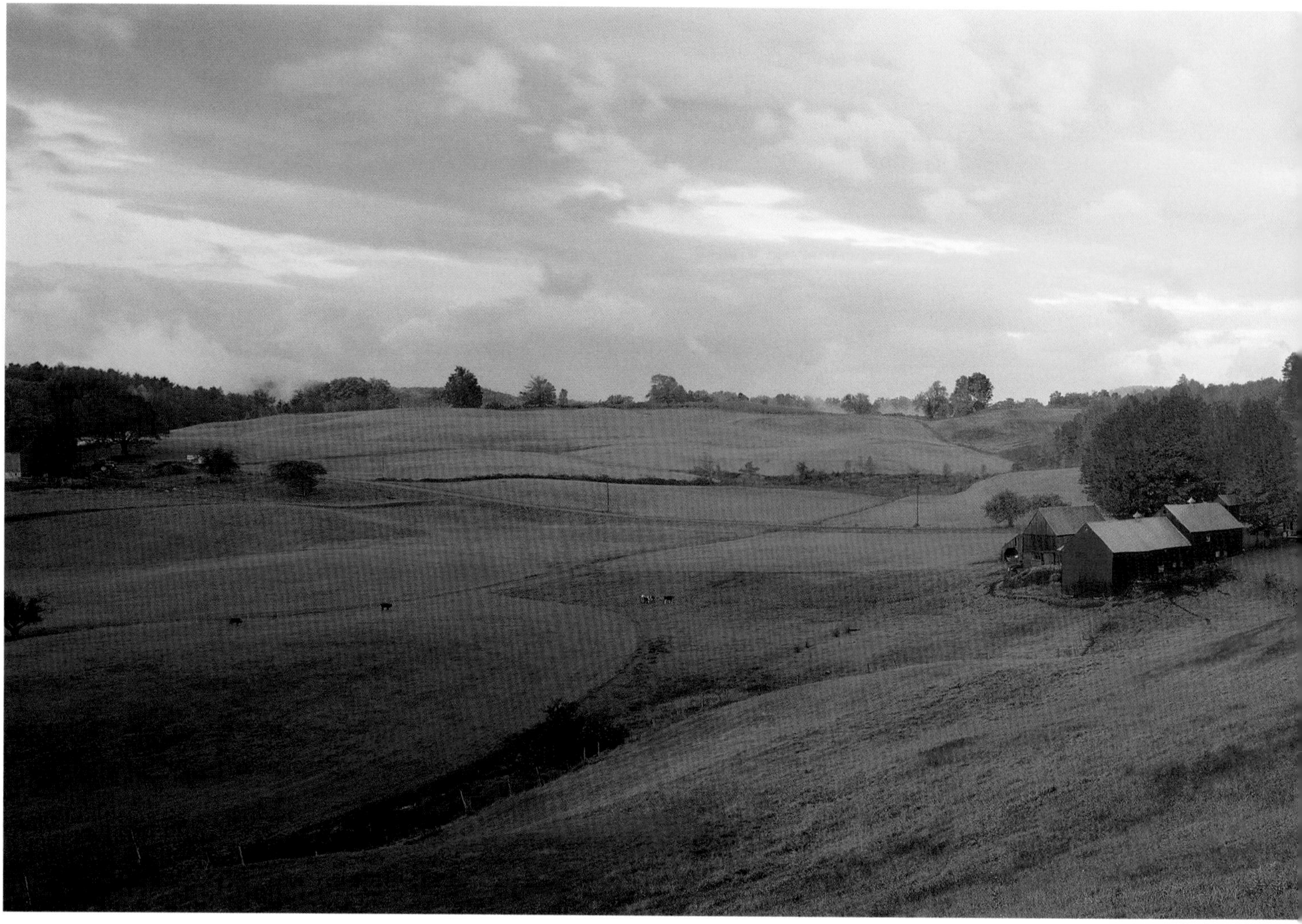

STAND FAST THEREFORE in the liberty by which

Christ has made us free,

and do not be entangled again with a yoke of bondage.

—GALATIANS 5:1

Jenne Farm, Woodstock, Vermont

Beautiful Vermont had trouble earning its statehood. The region was a point of significant contention by England, New York, New Hampshire, and Vermonters themselves. During the early days of the American Revolution, the area's status was still in question, so in 1777 the locals declared themselves the Vermont Republic. Their constitution was the first public document in the Americas to outlaw slavery. It also promoted free education for residents and granted voting privileges to more men. Vermont remained independent until 1791, when it finally was admitted to the union as the fourteenth U. S. state. Self-determination and an independent spirit are still two of the main attributes of the American character. God values self-determination, too, as He gives us each the freedom to either choose or reject Him.

Vermont

SING, O HEAVENS!

Be joyful, O earth!

And break out in singing, O mountains!

For the LORD has comforted His people,

And will have mercy on His afflicted.

ISAIAH 49:13

Vermont

One of Vermont's most famous families of the twentieth century was the Trapp family of *The Sound of Music* fame. In the movie, they hiked over the mountain at night to escape Nazi-occupied Austria; in reality they formed a traveling choir and sought a new life in America, far from the dangers plaguing Europe. They eventually settled in Stowe, Vermont. America has always been a haven for people from around the world who've needed a fresh start, and the country is richer for their presence and their many contributions.

MOSS GLEN FALLS, VERMONT

TO EVERYTHING THERE IS A SEASON,

A time for every purpose under heaven:

A time to be born,

And a time to die;

A time to plant,

And a time to pluck what is planted.

ECCLESIASTES 3:1-2

Autumn Colors, Woodstock, Vermont

Beautiful Vermont—here in its autumn glory. Every season has a beauty of its own. How boring life would be without seasons, for it is the contrast that gives texture to our lives. Autumn removes the old growth. Winter is a time of rest. Spring brings forth new life, and summer is a time for rejoicing.

Of all the dispositions and habits which lead to political prosperity, religion and morality are indispensable supports. In vain would that man claim the tribute of patriotism, who should labor to subvert these great pillars of human happiness, these firmest props of the duties of men and citizens. . . . Let us with caution indulge the supposition that morality can be maintained without religion. Whatever may be conceded to the influence of refined education on minds of peculiar structure, reason and experience both forbid us to expect that national morality can prevail in exclusion of religious principle. It is substantially true that virtue or morality is a necessary spring of popular government.

—*George Washington, U. S. President (1789-1797)*
Born 1732 in Westmoreland County, Virginia

White Oak Falls, Shenandoah National Park, Virginia

YET I WILL REJOICE in the LORD,

I will joy in the God of my salvation.

The LORD God is my strength;

He will make my feet like deer's feet,

And He will make me walk on my high hills.

HABAKKUK 3:18-19

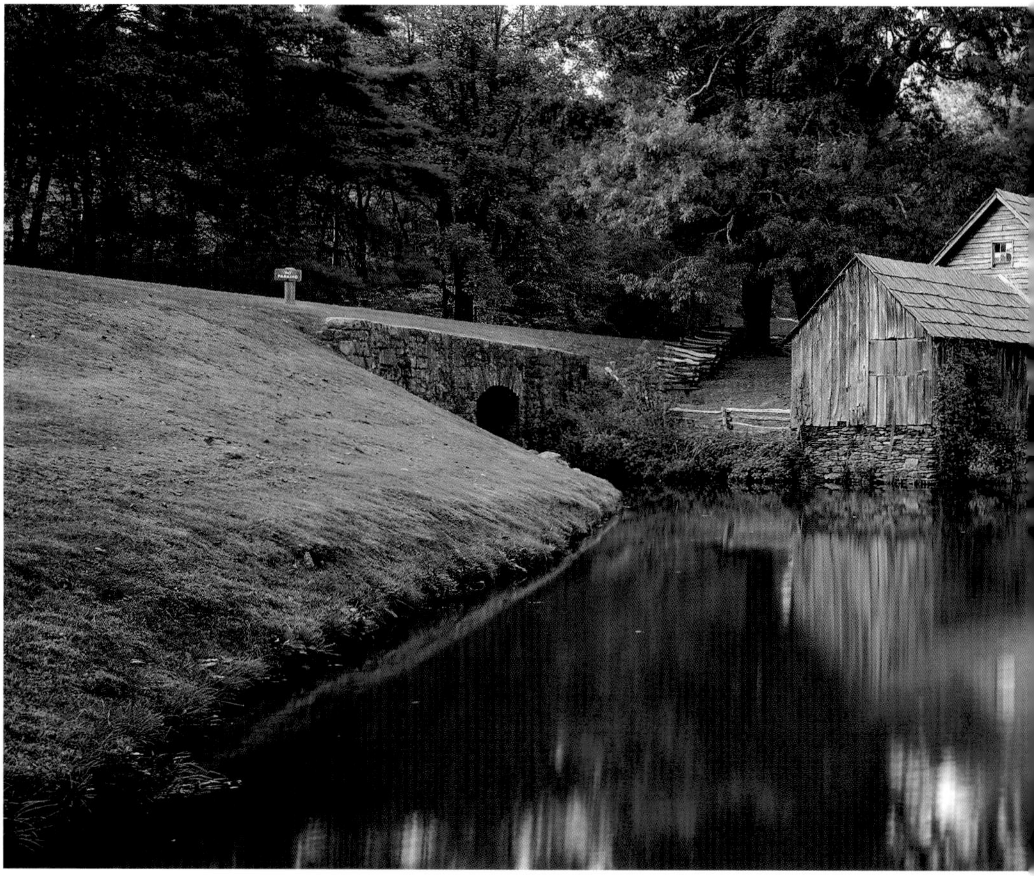

TWO MEN WILL BE IN THE FIELD:

one will be taken and the other left.

Two women will be grinding at the mill: one will be taken and the other left.

Watch therefore, for you do not know what hour your Lord is coming.

MATTHEW 24:40-42

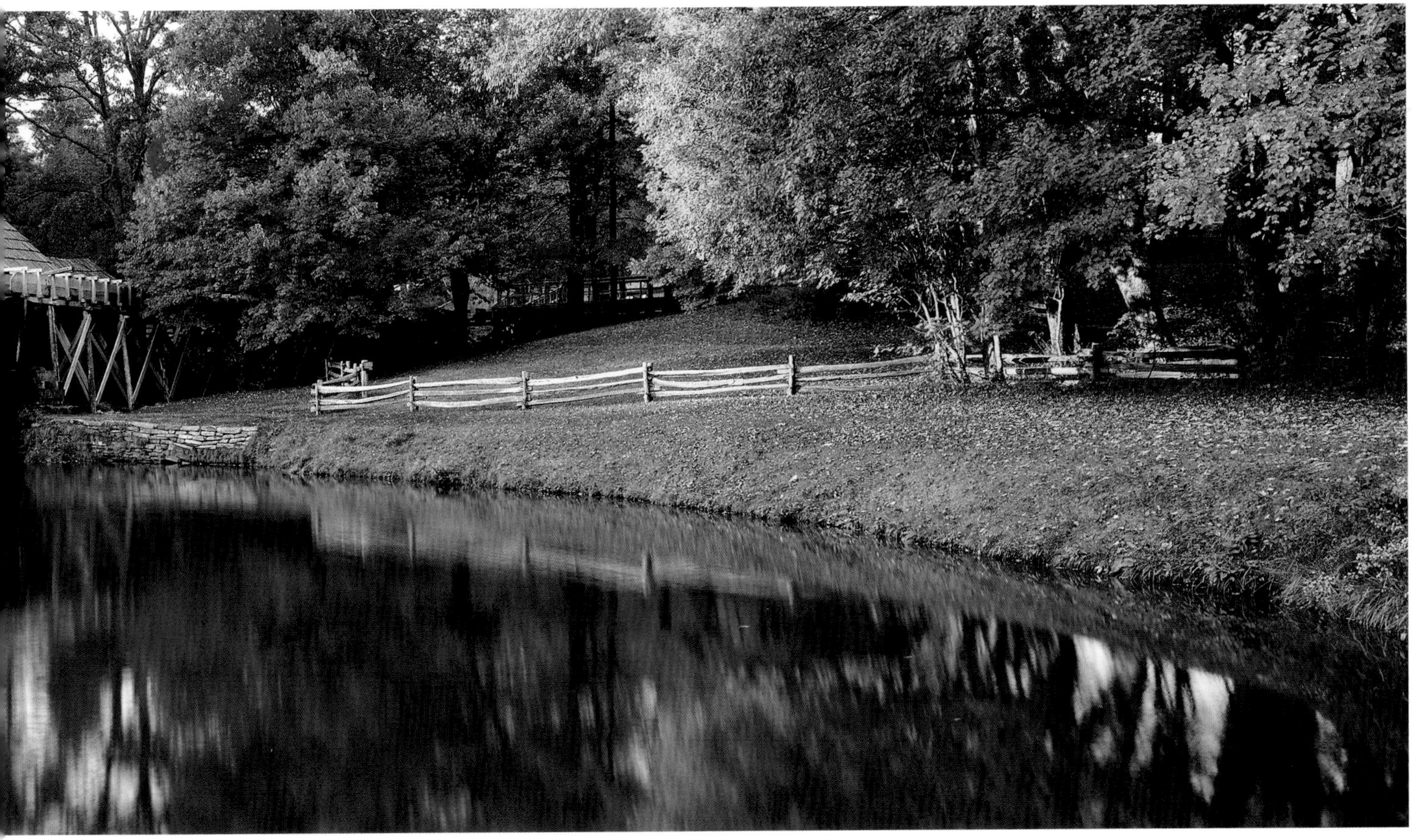

Mabry Mill, Blue Ridge Parkway, Virginia

The Mabry Mill stands as a monument to the enduring spirit of the mountain people. It was constructed in the early 1900s by a man whose family had owned the property for more than a hundred years. He built it in order to harness the stream's power for his many businesses. After Ed Mabry died, the mill eventually became a tourist attraction for demonstrating pioneer mountain life. Sometimes a sight like this time-tested, beautiful mill will remind me of the fact that no matter how hard you work in this life to build success, you can't take it with you. Others in the future may admire your life or accomplishments, but your part is done. You only have a short span—just one lifetime of an unknown quantity of days—to do anything that matters. Be sure to make Jesus a priority.

THOSE WHO ARE PLANTED in the house of the LORD

Shall flourish in the courts of our God.

They shall still bear fruit in old age;

They shall be fresh and flourishing,

To declare that the LORD is upright;

He is my rock, and there is no unrighteousness in Him.

PSALM 92:13-15

Daffodil Sunset, Skagit Valley, Washington

While photographing this field of vibrant flowers I saw some unused plows off to the side. The implements had great character developed by aging and rust, but they no longer served any real purpose. Later that afternoon I passed a freshly turned field, and the plow responsible for that fine job sat proudly in the furrows, its disks shining like mirrors reflecting the sun. In life we have choices. We can be like a disused plow—full of potential but not wanting to attach to the tractor of life and dig in deep. Or we can be like a burnished plow, constantly applying ourselves to the fields of our dreams so that our lives may shine and our dreams may take root and grow. If we allow the challenges of our lives to polish us for the tasks ahead, then one day we will reap a great harvest.

THE TESTING OF YOUR FAITH produces patience.
But let patience have its perfect work, that you may be perfect and complete,
lacking nothing. If any of you lacks wisdom, let him ask of God,
who gives to all liberally and without reproach, and it will be given to him.
But let him ask in faith, with no doubting, for he who doubts
is like a wave of the sea driven and tossed by the wind.

JAMES 1:2-6

Second Beach, Olympic National Park, Washington

Happiness and moral duty are inseparably connected.

—*George Washington,* U. S. President (1789-1797)

THE WORDS OF A MAN'S

mouth are deep waters;

The wellspring of wisdom is a flowing brook.

PROVERBS 18:2

Glade Creek Grist Mill, Babcock State Park, West Virginia

Everything has a season, and this view really testifies to that truth. I had heard that the trees here were spectacular in the autumn, so I had visited this mill many times to check foliage color. On my previous trips there had been little to see, but when I returned this day it seemed everything had come to its peak, just begging to be immortalized in an image.

Fall colors tinge this photograph with deep glory. The early morning sun has risen over the trees, and a wisp of mist washes the valley with coolness. The foreground is carpeted with crimson; a struggling fence, worn by the decades, leads to a traditional wooden homestead. This house is still occupied—a living memorial to the American pioneer spirit. It has seen much hard work through the seasons and the steady descent of generations. The reward, for the occupants, was a life lived far from the stress of the city. The beauty of nature was as close as their front door.

Pioneer Farm, Twin Falls State Park, West Virginia

"HE WHO BELIEVES IN ME,

believes not in Me but in Him who sent Me.

And he who sees Me sees Him who sent Me. I have come as a light into the world,

that whoever believes in Me should not abide in darkness.

JOHN 12:44-46

Lower Potato River Falls, Wisconsin

It is the sweet, simple things of life which are the real ones after all.

—*Laura Ingalls Wilder,* author, born 1867 in Pepin, Wisconsin

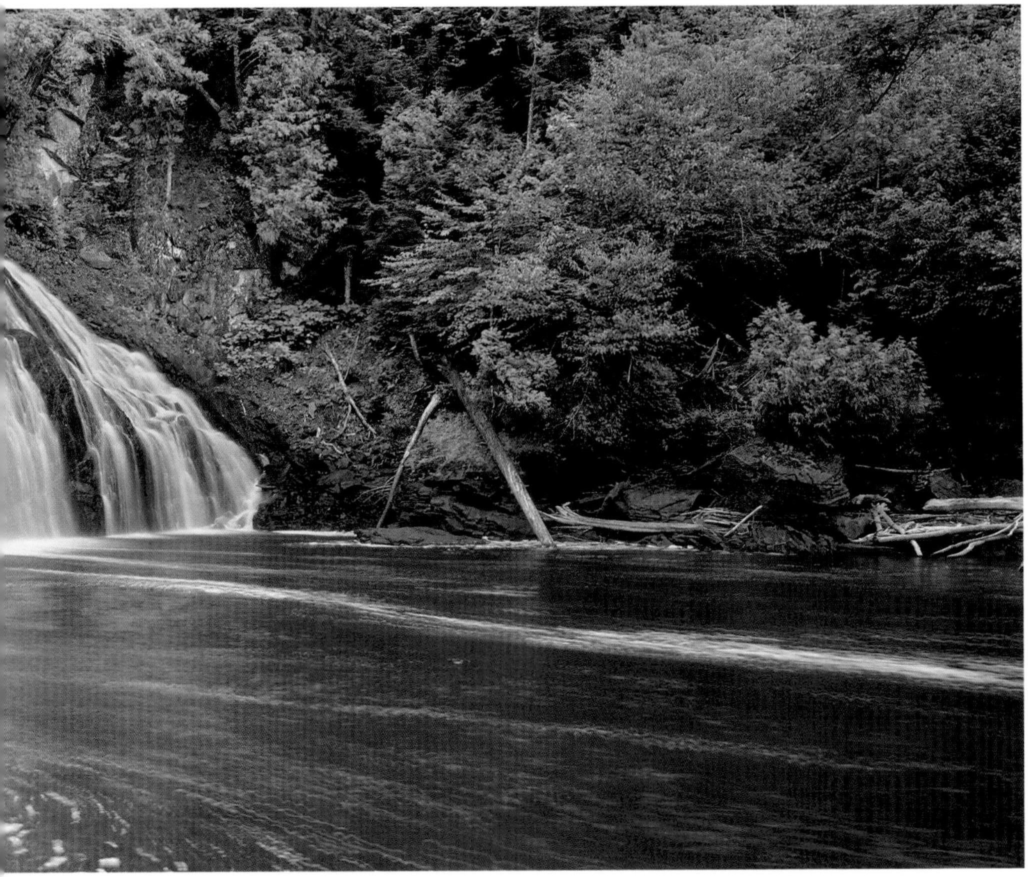

YOU DIVIDED the earth with rivers.

The mountains saw You and trembled;

The overflowing of the water passed by.

The deep uttered its voice,

And lifted its hands on high. . . .

Yet I will rejoice in the LORD,

I will joy in the God of my salvation.

HABAKKUK 3:9-10, 18

Wisconsin

BE ANXIOUS FOR NOTHING,

but in everything by prayer and supplication,

with thanksgiving, let your requests be made known to God;

and the peace of God, which surpasses all understanding,

will guard your hearts and minds through Christ Jesus.

PHILIPPIANS 4:6-7

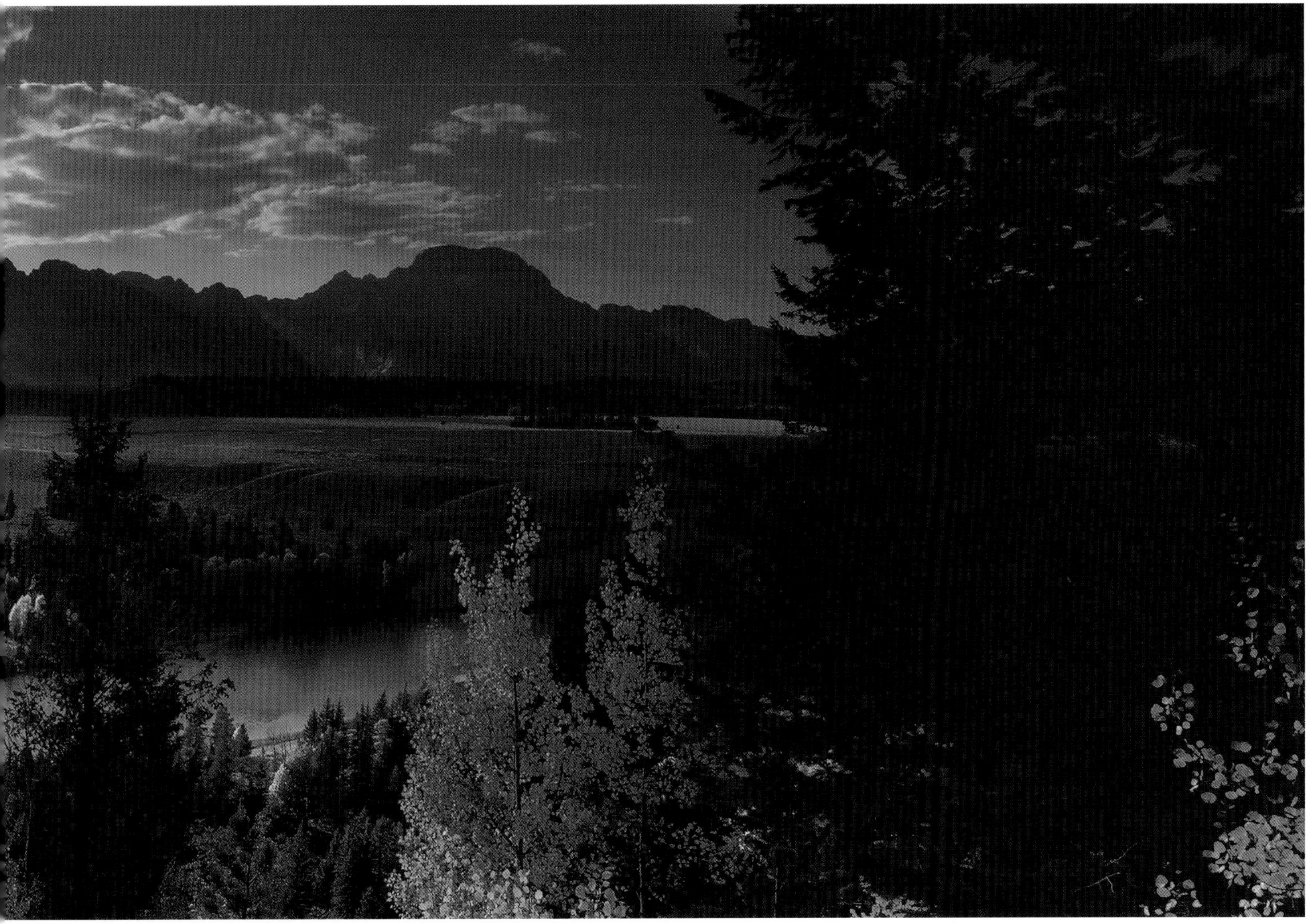

SNAKE RIVER, GRAND TETON NATIONAL PARK, WYOMING

I deem the present occasion sufficiently important and solemn to justify me in expressing to my fellow citizens a profound reverence for the Christian religion and a thorough conviction that sound morals, religious liberty, and a just sense of religious responsibility are essentially connected with all true and lasting happiness; and to that good Being who has blessed us by the gifts of civil and religious freedom, who watched over and prospered the labors of our fathers and has hitherto preserved to us institutions far exceeding in excellence those of any other people, let us unite in fervently commending every interest of our beloved country in all future time.

—*William Henry Harrison,* U. S. President (1841-1841)

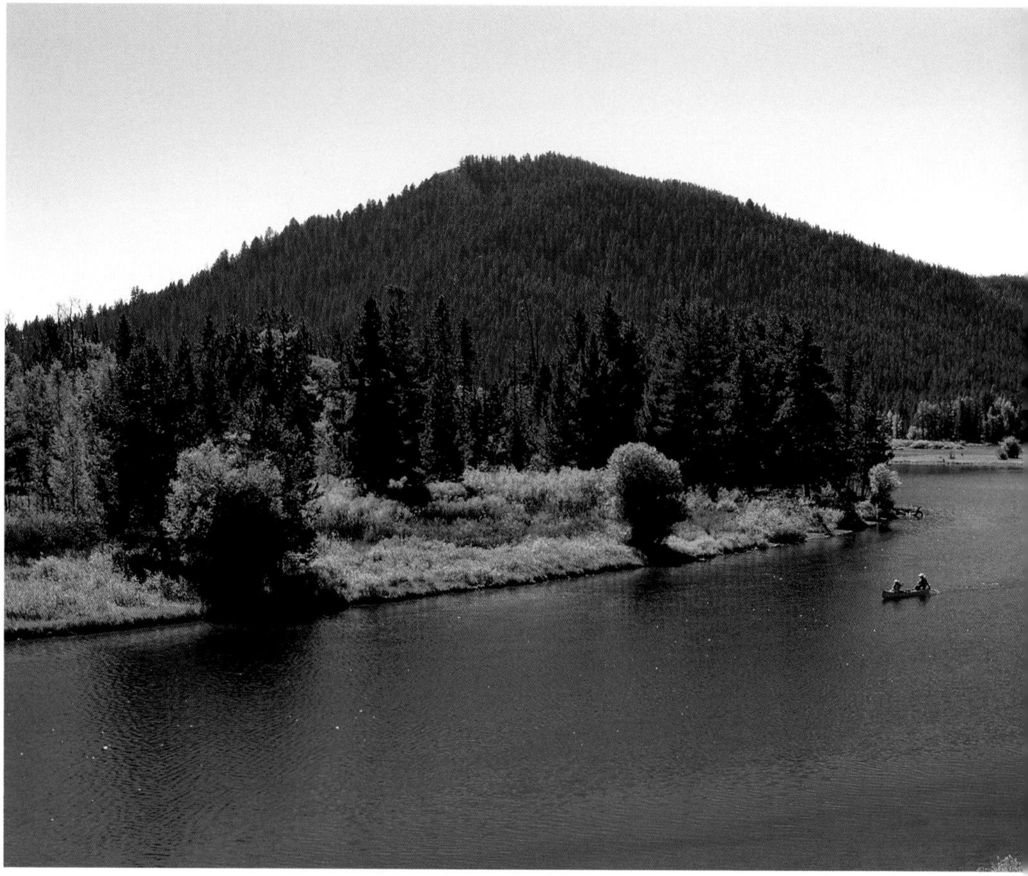

HOW PRECIOUS is Your lovingkindness, O God!

Therefore the children of men put their trust under the shadow of Your wings.

They are abundantly satisfied with the fullness of Your house,

And You give them drink from the river of Your pleasures.

For with You is the fountain of life;

In Your light we see light.

PSALM 36:7-9

Oxbow Bend, Grand Teton National Park, Wyoming

Wyoming needed help. The territory needed more votes on its quest for statehood, but there just weren't enough people who could vote. So, in 1869, it became the first place in America to extend suffrage to women. This made the territory an inspiration for some social reformers and the object of ridicule for others, but this form of equality between the sexes eventually came to be accepted as normal in the region. When statehood finally seemed imminent, the U. S. Congress threatened to block Wyoming's entry to the union unless women's suffrage was abolished, but local leaders refused to cave. In 1890, voting rights intact, Wyoming became the 44th state. The lesson here: Hold on to what you value.

EXALT THE LORD OUR GOD,

And worship at His holy hill;

For the LORD our God is holy.

PSALM 99:9

Chapel of the Transfiguration, Grand Tetons, Wyoming

This famous chapel built in 1925 is said to be the most visited religious structure in America. Nestled in dude ranch country, the chapel was an expression of faith shared by the early settlers of the valley. A large window behind the altar allows worshipers at this chapel to gaze upon the magnificent Grand Tetons. The mountains are a sermon in themselves, speaking volumes about the majesty of the Creator. In this sunrise shot, a delicate dusting of snow adds further charm to an already beautiful scene. At first the light here was dull, obscured by wild and swirling cloud overhead. But then there was a break in the sky, and the scene was briefly flooded with this heavenly light. I love the imagery of this shot—the open chapel situated in the midst of nature's splendor, inviting passersby to worship the God who made it all.

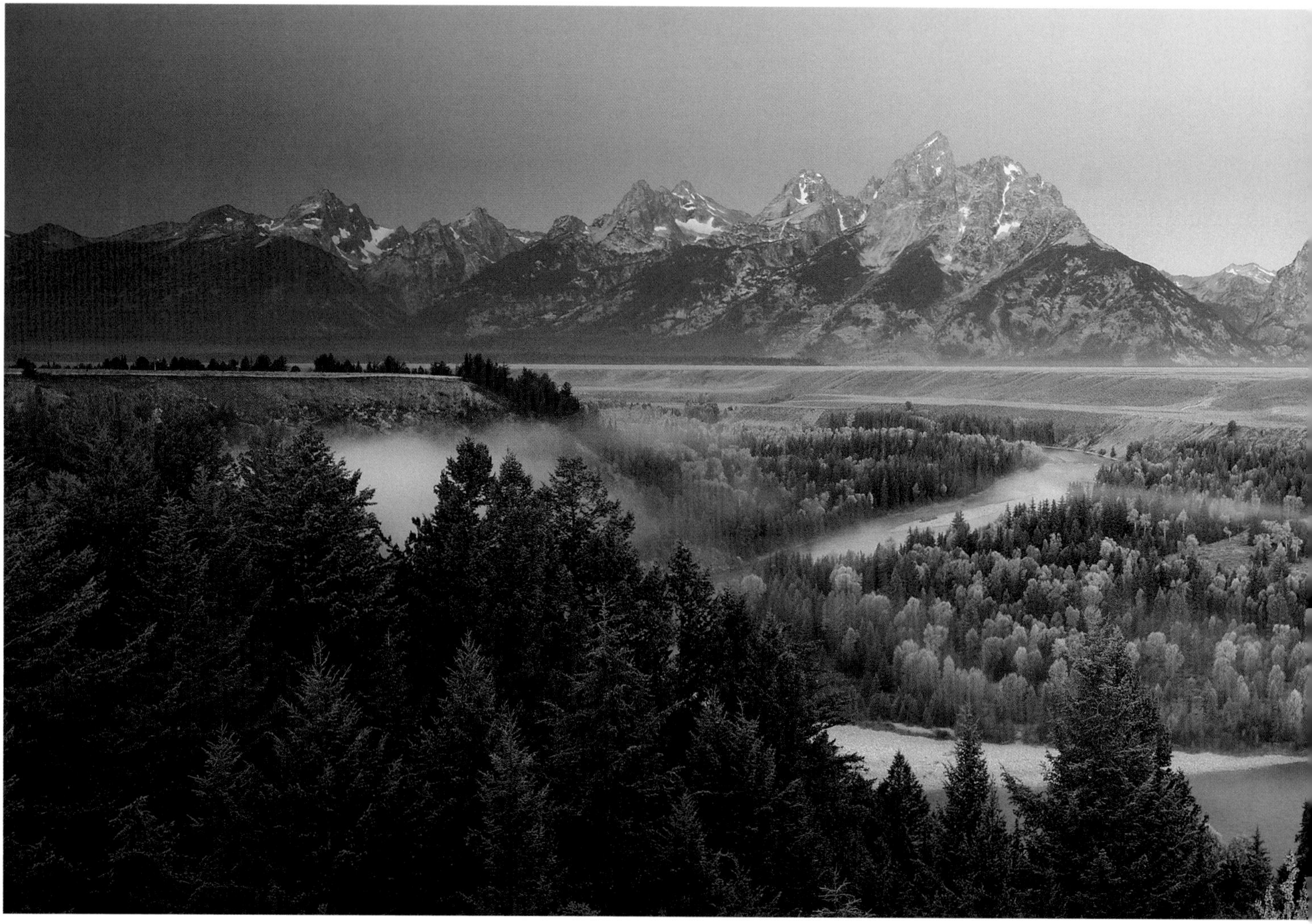

ONE GENERATION shall praise Your works to another,
And shall declare Your mighty acts.
I will meditate on the glorious splendor of Your majesty,
And on Your wondrous works.
Men shall speak of the might of Your awesome acts,
And I will declare Your greatness.
They shall utter the memory of Your great goodness,
And shall sing of Your righteousness.

PSALM 145:4-7

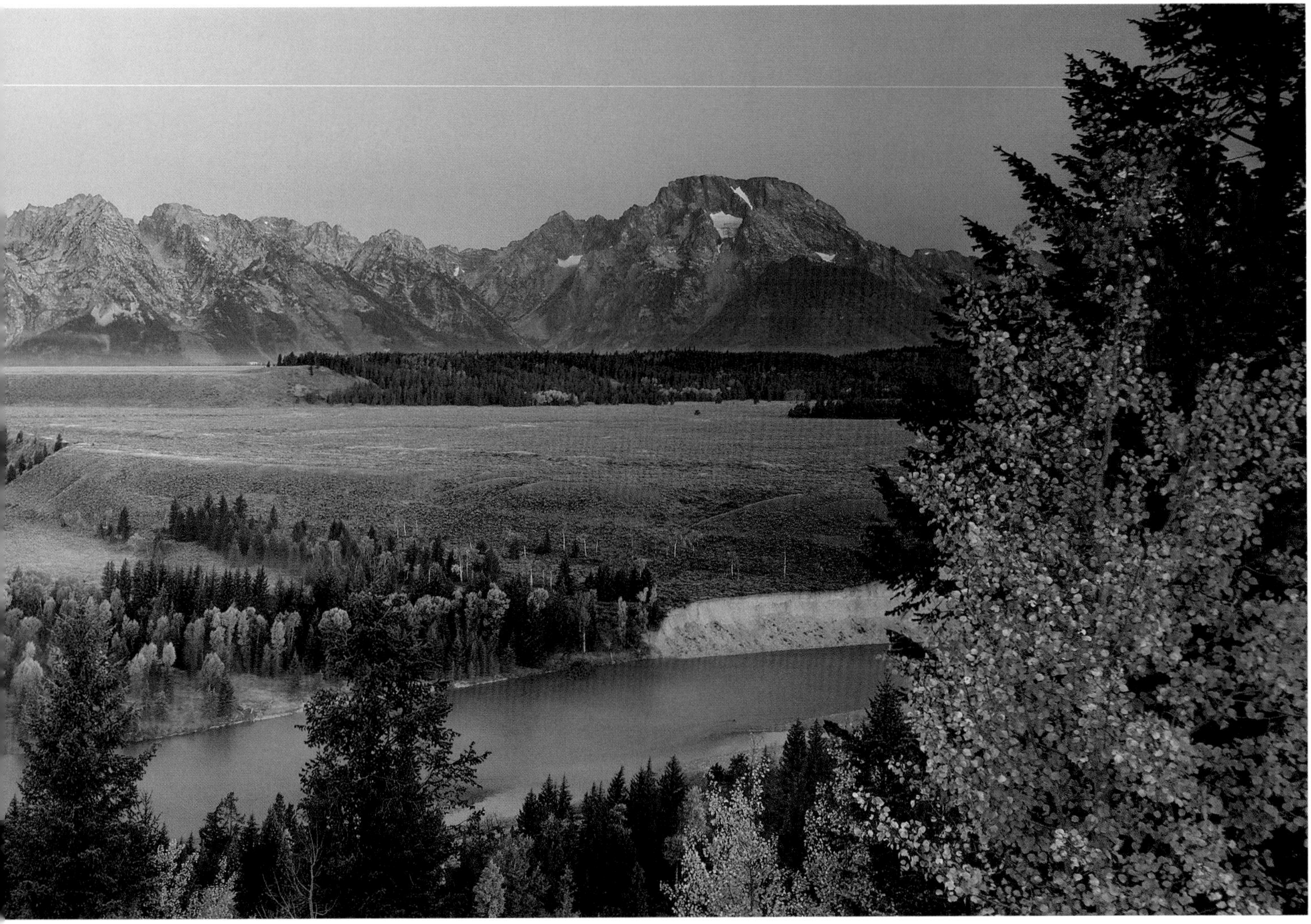

Snake River, Grand Teton National Park, Wyoming

Wyoming, a vacationer's outdoor paradise—Yellowstone National Park, Grand Teton National Park, Jackson Hole, dude ranches, and cowboys. Family memories are made in this rugged state. One of the most famous attractions is the Old Faithful geyser in Yellowstone. It spews warm water out of the earth about every eighty minutes, with plumes up to 184 feet. Perhaps your family has loaded up the car and driven untold hours across the country to see this and the other natural wonders of the West. But always remember that these natural wonders were devised by a supernatural, loving God, who created the world for both our use and enjoyment. Praise Him!

Matanuska Glacier, Alaska

Conclusion

I love America. Although it is not my country of citizenship, in a sense it is the nation of my ideals, and countless others around the globe feel the same way. America is blessed! Blessed! And by its very existence it continues to offer hope to all people who are "yearning to breathe free."

God told me to come photograph America. He showed me its glory, and He showed me how dearly He loves it. He also showed me that the nation will face ever-greater challenges to receiving His favor. The growing darkness is trying to prevent Jesus from shining throughout the land.

I pray that through this book you've seen anew the beauty of the United States and realize that America's greatness is a gift from God. Don't take God's blessings for granted. Remember, "For everyone to whom much is given, from him much will be required; and to whom much has been committed, of him they will ask the more" (Luke 12:48), and start looking for more ways to fulfill your responsibility to your neighbors both at home and around the world.

America is a priceless heritage and an awesome legacy for the future. May God give the nation's people the heart to love her, the wisdom to guide her, and the indomitable spirit to steward her in faith until Christ's return to establish and rule His perfect Kingdom. Amen.

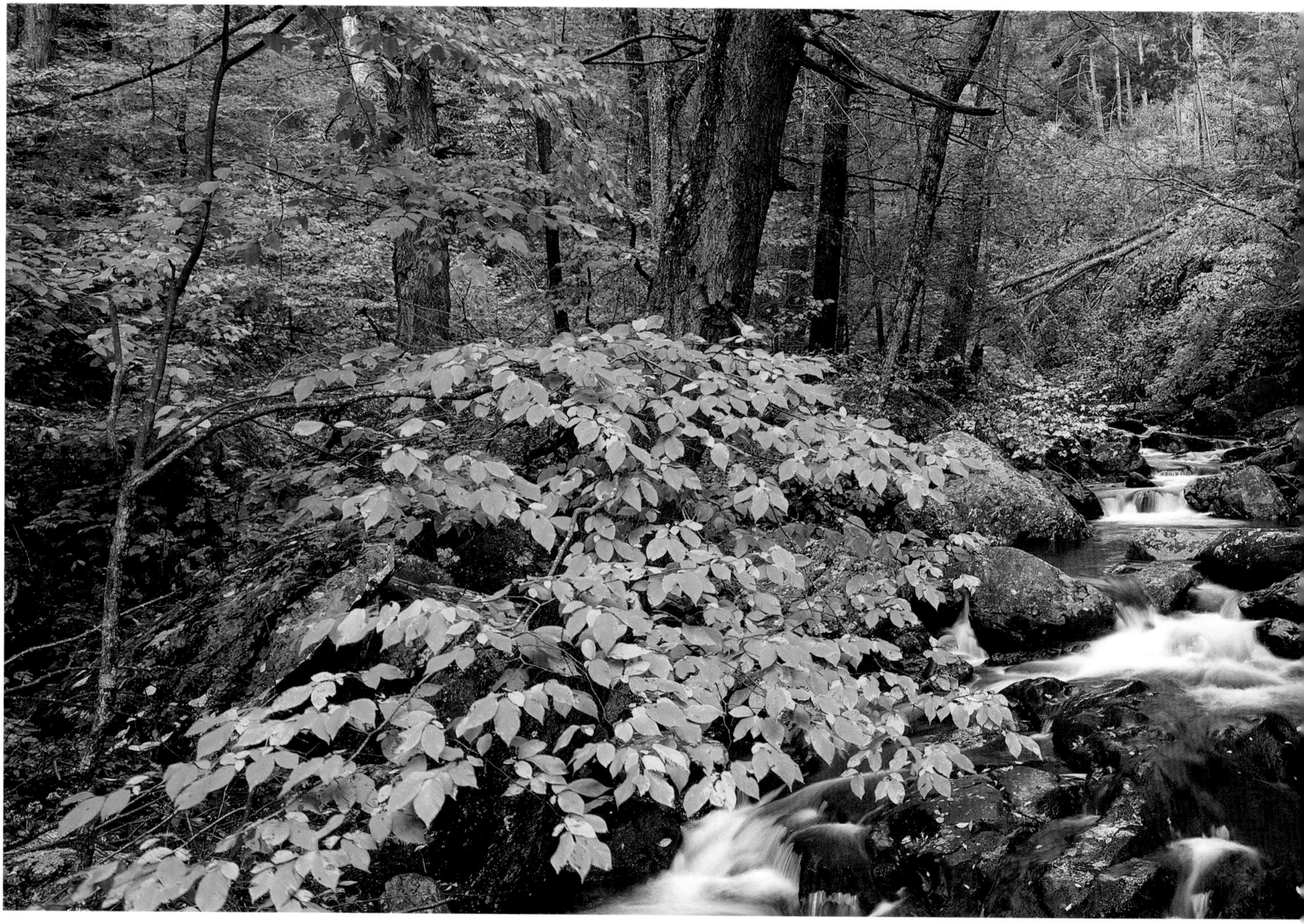

Photography Notes

Although people often contact me asking for photographic advice, I do not generally presume to tell anyone how to take photographs. I believe we all see differently and that is what gives each of us our unique style. When we follow our minds we are limited in our own understanding, but when we follow our hearts we see the bigger picture. Having said that, there are a few tips I can pass on.

Break the Rules

The bottom line is: there are no rules. If an image works, it works; if it doesn't, it doesn't.

Stop Talking and Start Taking

One of the hardest parts of photography is getting out of bed. Just stick a film in your camera and get on with it. If you have a dream to shoot a book on America, you can think of the immensity of the country and be so overwhelmed that you never begin. Or you can pick somewhere to start and attack it one bite at a time. If you persevere, you'll reach your goal.

White Oak Canyon Trail, Shenandoah National Park, Virginia

Looking Past The "I"

Often the biggest thing blocking the light is the shadow of our own intentions. We can get so locked into what we want to achieve or why we have gone to a particular area that we miss the very thing we are there for. I believe there is a force at work much bigger than us. The key is to tap into the Creator's power rather than your own technical understanding, which by comparison is very limited. This is a hard pill for many to swallow (especially "techno-heads") because people love to be in control. Personally, I would rather be out of control. I'm just an average photographer with a great God. I have definitely not perfected this area of relinquishing control, but I'm working on it. It's exciting! How small we are and how big He is!

Using What You Have

Many people think they need a better camera to take better photos—and it certainly is nice to have a great camera—but you'll improve more if you do more with the camera you have now. The best understanding of your equipment comes from using it.

Wild Light

Light is one of the most important things to consider. No light, no photograph! Early morning and late afternoon are generally the best times to take photographs as the light has great warmth and softness. One thing to be careful of is "blue sky mentality." Certain parts of America are blessed with lots of blue skies and this can sometimes become boring in photographs. Cloudy light or wild, moody light can test your patience, but when the break happens, you can get great emotion in a shot. Times of wild light are often when I speak to God asking (respectfully!) such things as, "What are You up to?" or " Come on, give me a break—please!"

The Third Dimension

Photography is a two dimensional medium, so we sometimes need to create the illusion of a third dimension in our photographs—especially in landscapes—to give depth to the images. A simple way to do this is to use strong foreground interest. Another way is to use lines within the shot to draw in the viewer—a road, a fence, a curve of beach. Sometimes a good way to get better depth in a photo is to shoot from a higher vantage point.

Crabtree Falls, Blue Ridge Parkway, North Carolina

Passion

Passion, like attitude, is contagious and is essential for a project to succeed. Life is an adventure, not a worry, and if you want to pursue a dream, stumbling blocks must become stepping stones. Passion is a powerful thing and when directed properly it can help bring visions to reality.

Patience

Patience can be a difficult discipline, but when we learn to be still, blessings come our way. Once I was shooting in Yosemite National Park and I waited all day for the light to be "just right." Throughout the day, about five other professional-looking photographers came along. Each one pulled out his mega-expensive camera, tripod, the works, waited a couple of minutes, then clicked off a few shots before leaving. Meanwhile, I was still waiting, waiting, waiting—wondering if in fact I had missed something. Finally, right at the end of the day, the light began to dance and the scene came alive.

For more information about photography and my photos, visit www.kenduncan.com.

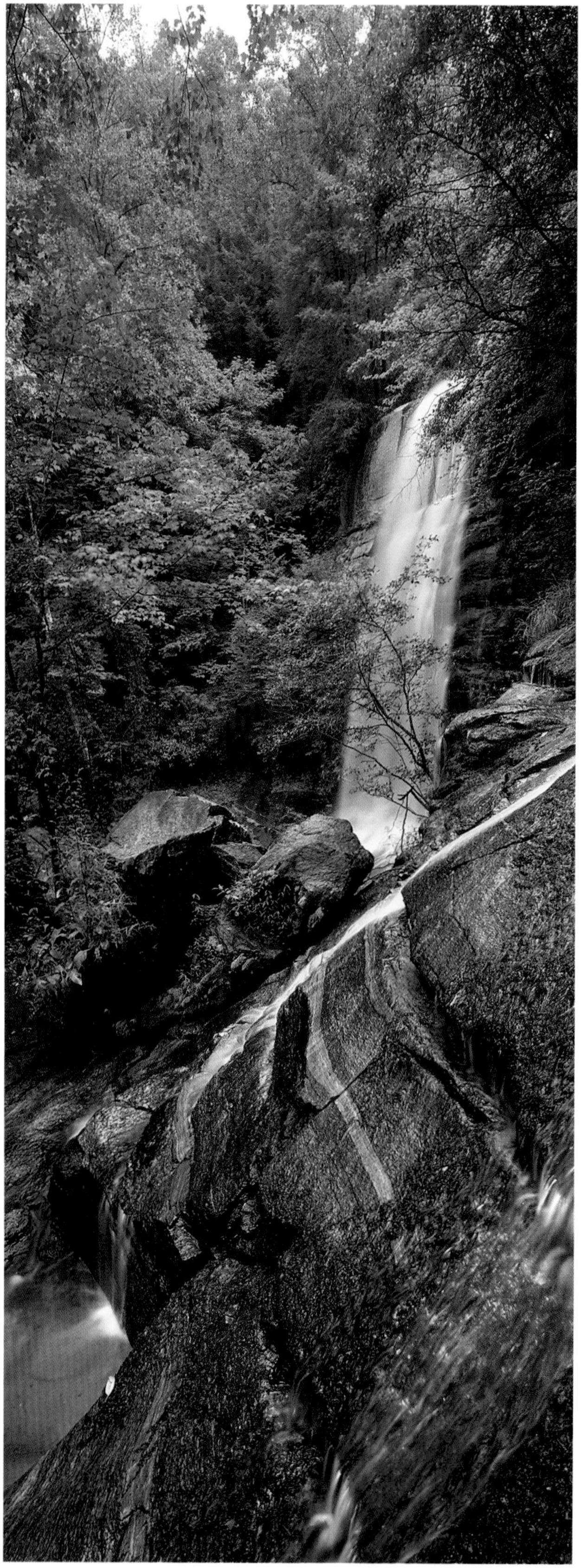

AMERICA IS GREAT

because she is good.

If America ceases to be good,

America will cease to be great.

—*Alexis de Tocqueville,*
French author of *Democracy in America* (1835)

COVE FALLS, REEDY RIVER, SOUTH CAROLINA